REAL ESTATE INVESTING:
A QUICK START GUIDE TO STARTING YOUR REAL ESTATE EMPIRE

Table of Contents

Real Estate Investing: 1
A QUICK START GUIDE TO STARTING YOUR REAL ESTATE EMPIRE 1
Chapter 1: How to Find Houses 5
Chapter 2: How to Buy Houses 7
Chapter 4: How to Sell Houses 19
Chapter 5: Success Stories 27
Chapter 6: Best Tools, Platforms, and Channels 29
Chapter 7: Basic Strategies 34
Chapter 8: Common Mistakes to Avoid 41
Chapter 9: Transitional Properties 80
Chapter 10: How to Sell the Finished Product 84
Chapter 11: Challenges to Property Flipping 89
Chapter 12: 10 Tips to Make the Most Money Flipping Houses 93
Chapter 13: Financing Your Business 98
Conventional Financing Options 98
Talk to Your Lender 104
Home Equity Line of Credit -- (HELOC) 105
Seller Financing 106
Raise the Price and Lower the Terms 107
Use Your Investment Property Inventory 108
Find an Investor 108
Use Your Commission 109
Lease Option 110
Trade for It 111
Your Family and Friends 111

Your Credit Rating 112
Watch Out for Pitfalls 117
Reason #1 118
Reason #2 120
Reason #3 121
What is Creating Wealth and What is Cash Flow? 124

Chapter 15: Types of Real Estate Investing 127
Purchasing Rental Properties 127
Lease Option 129
Why would a property owner want to sell by Rent-to-Own? 129
Home Buying 133
Renting 135
Rent-to-Own or Lease Option 136
Lease Option as an Investment Strategy 137
How do you protect yourself from these possibilities? 140
Hybrid Consumer 144
Risk versus Return on Investment 145
Icing on the Cake 147
Assignment of Contracts and Bank Short Sales 147
Tax Liens and Tax Deed Purchases 151
Building a New Home for Lease or Sale 154
The Appraisal 157
Do an "Arms Length" Appraisal 157
Rehabilitate a Resale Home and Sell for Profit 158
Building Your Resource Team 166

Chapter 16: Finding a "Good Deal" 167
What is your exit strategy? 168
What are your goals? 169
What are your skills? 170
What is your financial strength? 170

Your Company Weaknesses 175
Online Web site Promotion 176
Budget 177

Chapter 17: Doing a Buy/Sell Analysis 178
Easy Math 178
The Closest Thing to a Crystal Ball 189
If You Want the Cash 195

Chapter 18: Review Your Business Plan 198
Tax Benefits 205
Ordinary and Necessary Expenses 206
Education Expenses 209
Legal and Professional Fees 209
Bad Debts 210
Business Entertaining 211
Travel 211
Taxes 212
Advertising and Promotion 214
Easily Overlooked Business Expenses 215

Conclusion 217

Chapter 1: How to Find Houses

This chapter will guide you in learning about the best resources available to get the best properties to flip for a good profit. Flipping real estate is a reference to purchasing properties for a small fee, fixing the home up, and then selling it to make a profit. Prospecting or understanding the best places where to look is a crucial element in this flipping process.

Realtor.com

This site will match you to properties that fit your criteria and then offer up the realtor information so that you can meet with them to check out the property and potentially purchase it. You can use this also to find a realtor to partner with on your flipping ventures. This site offers you advanced searches; therefore, you can input a maximum price so that you can ensure that you are not spending too much of your flipping budget.

Trulia

Trulia is realtors that are selling, much like realtor.com, but you can find different properties from "for sale by owner." It offers information that you will need so that you can decide if this is the property you would like to purchase.

Zillow

Zillow provides information about every piece of property listed for sale by the owner or Realtor Company. You can do an advanced search to find the house that you would like to begin flipping. Keep in mind that you can live in the home while you flip it.

Chapter 2: How to Buy Houses

There are many different avenues to find discounted properties to flip. In this chapter, we are going to dive into various options that are available; from working with different types of attorneys to finding probate properties. Keep in mind that you can use multiple avenues to pick up properties and are not limited to one.

Finding Leads for the Properties

You will need access to the Multiple Listing Service, also known as MLS. This database has all the houses that are for sale, whether they are listed under contract by a real estate agent or by any other broker. The realtor can set up a search for the listing requirements that you want to bring up a list of potential homes to flip. For example, if you were to express that you are looking for homes that are three bedrooms or more with two bathrooms, as well as a specific amount of square footage, he or she will be able to bring up a list. The search can even include maximum pricing, amenities, and much more. You are even able to set a particular build year. They will also be able to bring up a list of foreclosures that you can flip.

Find Leads for the Properties

You should join a real estate group. It will put you right in the middle of all the local real estate associated individuals. It will also give you a chance to speak with those that are in the group, where you can talk up the next project that you plan to conduct. Typically, there will be someone that will have a project that they need a partner on or you will find someone that will partner with you on your project.

You can also hear about different properties that an investor is trying to unload because they do not have time to flip it or they need a quick turnaround. You can make many friends and network with valuable associates in this group. To find the group, do a simple Google search in your area.

Check Out Tax Auctions

These tax auctions are to auction off properties that have not paid their taxes. This is an excellent way to find unusual properties that you can flip. To get a property of this nature, you will have to pay the unpaid taxes to take over ownership of the home. You can find when and where the auctions are by visiting the local website for the county or the city. Before the sale of the home, you will need first to register as an auction bidder. Sales are made to the public and buyers will have the opportunity to bid on the properties. You may want to consult an attorney before the auction. The attorney should be the one that is representing the financial institutions of which the properties are being purchased.

Contact Wholesalers

Wholesalers are companies that will typically acquire the properties through the tax sales or even short sales and then sell them to investors. These companies typically have many buyers that are looking to flip houses, hold them, or even buy them for personal reasons. Once they have acquired the property, the home wholesaler will then write a description of the property.

Local Papers

Many people still list homes for sale in the newspaper. They will put out ads to sell their homes. You will more than likely find an "Open House" ad, which typically list when and where it will be. You can find many mobile homes and even condominiums that are for sale by the owner, also known as FSBO.

Estate Sales and Probate Sales

Real Estate Investing

Estate sales and probate sales are an excellent way to purchase homes to flip. They are typically in decent shape and have a discounted price. Probate sales are those properties that are being sold by the probate court due to the owner not having a will or don't have heirs. This is a more advanced system for acquiring homes, but it is a way to get homes at a discounted price. You will need to place a 10% nonrefundable deposit, so if you don't close the deal, you lose the deposit. Also, the seller disclosures about the defects are not required.

Send Mail to Absentee Property Owners

If you come across a run-down home, and you believe that it may be a rental, then you can find the name of that particular owner using the town clerk. You can even read the obituary section in a newspaper for the leads on different homes that may need to be sold due to death. You can send a letter offering to buy the home. Use the website whitepages.com to find the address of the homeowner and those who may have taken over ownership.

Work with a Probate Attorney for the Potential Homes

You can partner up with a probate attorney. These types of lawyers collaborate with the families that are going through the process of probate to liquidate assets like cars, houses, bonds, stocks, and more. Networking with a probate attorney will open up a new path to flipping for wealth with close to no competition on purchasing the property.

Work with a Divorce Attorney

Partnering with a divorce attorney can help you become a successful flipper. Many couples decide that their marriage should end. They typically have a property that is required to be sold to split the profits to be fair. You will be there to pick up the home at a discounted price. You will then be able to flip the home for a profit.

Chapter 3: How to Renovate

The trick to flipping homes is to get them updated and sell them so that you can make a profit. However, if you put a lot of money into the home, you will not make as much profit as would have been achieved if you had done the renovating in a smart way. In this chapter, you are going to learn how to renovate without going past budget and make a larger profit in return.

The Kitchen

The kitchen is the most important part of the home to potential buyers. If you do not have enough funds to redo a kitchen completely, do not worry. You can spend $1,000 to make larger and more significant changes that will have the buyers putting in the bids.

- *Refinishing or refacing cabinets*: Refacing the cabinets means that you will replace the cabinet doors, but you will leave the cabinet boxes intact. Depending on the size of the kitchen, you may be able to get it done for approximately $1,000 by a professional, or you can save some money by doing it yourself. If the cabinet doors are wood, then you can refinish them by stripping off the old paint or the varnish and put on new. The refinishing will cost around $300.

- *Changing the Countertops*: Depending on the size of the kitchen, you can purchase new countertops made of granite for approximately $1,000. At times you can even find it for about $40 per square foot. For those kitchens that are larger, you can get steel. If you are used to doing this kind of work, then you can even make countertops for about $50.

- *Painting Rooms*: With one gallon of paint you can cover about 350 square feet. The average cost of one gallon of paint will cost about $25. Add in the cost of primer and brushes and you will be able to paint the kitchen for about $75 for a brand new and fresh look.

- *Updating the Accessories*: Small changes like replacing the cabinet knobs, outlet covers, and drawer pulls will give the kitchen an entirely different look. Once you consider the size of the average kitchen, you can upgrade all these for about $150..

- *Tiling Floors*: Studies show that people prefer ceramic tile. You can visit your local hardware or home improvement store for discounted tiles. These will cost you about $1 to $2 per square foot.

The Bathroom

After you have remodeled the kitchen, you should work on the bathroom. The great news is that according to one of the largest contractors, bathroom renovations will typically help to prompt a bid from a buyer up to about 80 to 90 percent more. For a smaller space, you can boost the sale by using about $1,000. You should re-tile the floor, update the tub or shower, and ensure the sink matches.

The Curb Appeal

There small changes that boost the homes curb appeal for the buyers. Here is what a budget of $1,000 will be able to do.

- *Add a Deck*: If you are a handyman, or you have some friends that will be able to help you, you should consider building a wooden deck to add to the home's outdoor living space. If you are not adding on an enormous deck, you can purchase the lumber and other necessary supplies to add a deck for a higher profit.
- *Replace Lawns*: This job can be done for about $1,000. The workers will rip up the lawn that is already there and replaces it with sod. It will

increase the value of the home. Make sure that you take care of it per the worker's instructions.

- *Entranceway*: You will draw the buyers to the front door with aesthetically pleasing planters, flowers, and a hardwood bench. You can add in a set of chairs and a patio table. Line your walkway with a border of plants and some small, simple lighting.

Upgrading Efficiency

There are some upgrades that you can do for the budget of about $1,000 to bring up the value and the appeal of the flipping home.

- *Tankless*: Installing a tankless water heater will cost anywhere from $150 to $1,000. It is an energy efficient upgrade for today's buyers. It will save you on the utility bills, so this is a significant upgrade that will wow the potential buyers.
- *Ceiling Fans*: Ceiling fans are not just to decorate a home. They are an easy way to reduce the energy consumption of the home during the summer months.

Replacing Appliances

There will be times that you would like to include a furnished kitchen. Items like refrigerators or ovens cost a lot when buying new. To increase value and save money, you should visit your local appliance store. They will have refurbished appliances that are like new. These will cost far less, but still give you the value that you are looking to add.

Chapter 4: How to Sell Houses

In this chapter we are going to cover how to sell houses; from how to find your potential buyers all the way to how to negotiate the price when the customer wants to haggle. It is advised to learn about these aspects to ensure that you know how to conduct business once the time comes.

How to Find Buyers

There are different ways to find your potential buyers. The first step is to enlist a Realtor. They will be able to find buyers and show them the property. They will deal with a lot of the transaction details for you; however, there are other options should you not want to use a realtor.

Another way to find your buyers is to conduct an open house. This is where potential buyers come to look at the home. You can put out an ad in the paper, list it online, and also put up signs around the city expressing when and where the open house takes place. This brings in potential buyers, as well as curious neighbors that will put the word out to their loved ones that they want next door.

How to Understand Buyers Needs and Preferences

Needs are statistical. The buyer will have the minimum bedroom requirements and other aspects of a home in mind. It is important to note that different families need different things. From hardwood flooring to wanting three bedrooms, the options on a home will change per person or family. There are some things to keep in mind when you flip a home. Flipping a home that has one bedroom will typically sell to a bachelor or a couple without kids. This will change what you will do to the home. A home that has three or more bedrooms will typically sell to a larger sized family. This means that if you fence in the yard, they will be more inclined to purchase the home due to the fence being a need for the children and animals that kids seem to acquire. Here are examples of needs and wants of the potential buyers.

Needs:

- Certain number of bedrooms.
- Certain number of bathrooms.
- Size and condition of kitchen.
- Access to good schools.
- Bigger yard size.
- Being close to a grocery store, library, or other establishment.

Wants:

- Floor Types
- Colors of Paint

- ***Pools***
- Hot Tubs
- Bay Windows
  - Entrance Chandelier

How to Negotiate Selling Prices

If you have not gone through the selling of a home yet, then there are some key points that you will need to keep in mind. First, understand that you should counter the list price. As the seller, you will be inclined to accept the buyer's first bid on the house. You should not. Buyers expect a back and forth type of negotiation. This means that the initial offer will be low. It will be much less than they expect to buy the house. This is a technique that buyers use to save some money on the home. You should counter the offer. This means to come down just a bit from the asking price of the home. They will then send another number your way. They send back a number that is higher than their previous offer due to being afraid that they will lose the opportunity to buy the property. The buyer and the seller should be flexible on the price. The trick here is to list the house higher than what you expect to sell.

Another way to do this is to counter offer with the original price that you have the house listed. Those who are genuinely interested in the house will stay in the negation game and send back an offer that is higher than their original offer. This will also show that you have listed the property for what it is worth. However, this will be done if you have listed the home for a fair price to begin with. Some sellers list the home much higher than it is worth to give room for negation without losing too much of the profit. Some sellers will only consider dropping the offer by $1,000 per counter offer.

Rejecting the Offer

Another way to negotiate is to reject the first offer and then invite the potential buyer to resubmit an offer. If you are gutsy, you can try this tactic. It is considered to be a bit more extreme over countering the offer. Just rejecting the offer and not countering it with an offer of your own will weed out the buyers that are not completely serious about purchasing the home. Also, when you reject the offer, it ensures that you are not locked into negotiations with one buyer. You can consider different offers from other buyers.

Real Estate Agents

If you do not feel confident in the negotiation process, may want to consider hiring a real estate agent that will help walk you through the process. They get their fee off the sale of the home, so you can be assured that they will be able to find common ground between you and the buyer. They want to sell the home to make their commission, but they do not want to sell it cheap because it will lower their commission. There is a fine line in between the seller and the buyer that the real estate agent will be able to find.

How to Stage a Home

When you are selling a house it is crucial that the property looks its best; inside and out. If you have a place to store items for staging, then you are able to use the same items for each home. But where would you get staging items without having to purchase brand new items for them to never be used? There are multiple places that you are able to stage on a budget.

- *Discount Retail Stores*: This is a great idea. A discount retail stores offer brand new items, but for a smaller price. They will even offer clearance items. Check out these stores around season change so that you will be able to get a lot of different items for a fraction of the price.
- *Thrift Stores*: Thrift stores are available in every town or city. It is like an all year yard sale. You are able to purchase used items that are like new. You can find rugs, furniture, and so much more that you can utilize to stage a home.
- *Yard Sales*: Yard sales are another amazing spot to get great staging items for a very small price. You can find furniture, home décor, and

so much more. If you find that there is an item that you would love to have as a staging item, then you can even haggle the price down some.

- *Estate Sales*: Estate sales are a bit better when it comes to finding staging furniture and home décor as an estate sale is when a person passes and their families are selling item due to them no longer being needed, whereas yard sales are families getting rid of things they have grown tired of.

When you are staging the home, remember to not pack it with a lot of items. A few tables, a couch, and maybe a lamp with a frame would be great for the living room. You should just enough furniture and décor to prompt their imagination of them living in this home.

Chapter 5: Success Stories

In this chapter, we are touching on a few success stories that were brought up in another one of the Real Estate Investing books offered. If you find that you can get your hands on a cheaper piece of property that is in decent repair, then you have a great beginning to your flipping business.

Ronnie Fields

Ronnie Fields began flipping when he was 25. He had a good idea of renting properties but ended up getting a great offer on his first property. He decided to take the offer, and thus began his extreme flipping business.

George Drake

George Drake was given property by an uncle that was passing away. After he had gotten the property, he had to relocate due to business. He decided that he was going to fix up the home and sell it. He found that he had a passion for it and used the profits to purchase another property and quit his job to become a successful flipper.

Diane Richardson

Diane had a passion for DIY projects and wanted to do a job out of it. However, she did not want it on a small level. She decided to purchase a small home that was next to her house and use her DIY skills to fix it up and then sold it for double of what she purchased. She found she loved this project and began to buy and sell a property approximately every six months. She was able to pay for her daughter college.

Chapter 6: Best Tools, Platforms, and Channels

There are many different tools, platforms, and channels that you can use to ensure the success of your flipping business. In this chapter, you are provided valuable information on aspects of flipping that you will be able to use. Keep in mind that you can utilize one or all of the information that is in this chapter.

BiggerPockets

This is an app that is available only on the iOS as of right now, but will be looking to expand to the Android soon. This app will allow you to engage in different forums quickly. You can ask and answer questions about the real estates that you have for sale. You are also able to reel in new properties to flip with this app. You can virtually be anywhere and still conduct business on getting new properties, as well as answering any questions of potential buyers.

MagicPlan

This is an app that will allow you to create floor plans by moving the phone or the iPad around any room and taking pictures. It will automatically map out the room. This is an amazing app for those who want to easily and quickly make up a floor plan. Those who are rehabbing can use it to make house plans before they begin to remodel and plan for the materials. You can record a virtual tour of a room. It is a great rehab and marketing tool for flippers.

Zillow

Zillow is not just a website, but they offer a free app for any device as well. This tool is a fantastic tool to have when you are a flipper. This app will show you what properties are available for purchase. This app offers a map that is very helpful when you are out driving to see the properties that need to be purchased and flipped. You can also see the sold properties in those areas. This helps find a good asking price for the home that you are flipping.

JotNot Scanner

JotNot is a very simple to use app that will allow you to turn your device into a portable scanner, and you can share the documents through email, DropBox, Evernote, Google Drive, and much more. This saves flippers the inconvenience of having to fax or copy documents, which can waste precious time. However, if you have this app, you will save a lot of time and money.

HammerPoint

This app is available for the iOS and will allow you to create detailed repair estimates for the jobs on a property. You can create new reports for each of the projects, and the app will walk you through them. It will auto fill descriptions of the work details and even offer you a suggested cost for a particular repair. You are also able to export the reports so that you can share and print them. This is a great tool for flippers to ensure that they are not going over budget on repairs, as well as prioritize the repairs based on budget.

Digital Receipts

This allows you to take a picture of receipts and email them so you stay organized and create the expense reports that you will need. This app will also help your business to be paperless and save money. Flippers should use this app due to a lot of the materials that are purchased being tax deductible. You have to have a receipt for this, though. This app will ensure that you always have the receipt and will not miss out on the money back when it is tax season.

Redfin

Redfin is a site that gives many listings of home that are for sale and offer virtual tours. You can enlist a real estate agent and so much more. You can use the search options to eliminate property types in which you are not interested.

Homes.com

Homes.com offers the same as the other two, but you are also able to find a realtor should you want to hire one for your property or properties. You can find real estate to purchase for flipping, or you can sell the one that you have already rehabbed.

Trulia

Trulia offers a channel for those who are buying and selling homes as well as checks out possible properties on the market. You can use this channel to find your flipping property, as well as sell the one you have ready to go. They offer an app for all types of devices.

Chapter 7: Basic Strategies

There are some basic strategies that you can utilize to sell houses successfully. In this chapter are seven strategies you can utilize to begin your flipping business. You will find that one property can be flipped using one of them, while another may use a different strategy altogether.

Standard Fix then Flip

This strategy is the most basic of strategies and the most widely used. This is the process that requires three steps. You will purchase the property. You will then renovate it, and then you will sell it at a higher price. While this is the most straightforward approach, it is also the most tried and true method and brings in the most profit.

Leasing Option

In this strategy, the first steps are the same. You will purchase the property and then you will fix it up. However, the third step in this process is different than the fix and flip. The third step is where you will rent the property out. The tenant will pay you upfront for the leasing option. This option will give the tenant a choice to purchase the property once their lease is over. If they do not want to buy it, you can find a different buyer and sell the property.

This strategy is fantastic to use when you would like to wait for the housing market to become much less competitive. If you purchase a house in the aggressive market, then you can lease it out and still make money while it sits. Then, once the market dies back down, you can sell it for a much higher profit than you would have gotten if you had used the first strategy.

Wholesaling Strategy

For those who are just beginning in the flipping game, you will need to start with a simple strategy, and this is a good one. You will be able to dip your toe in the flipping process right from the beginning.

Real Estate Investing

This is just like the first strategy, but you will not be doing any renovating.

Once you become a wholesaler, you will find a property below the market value, put this under contract, and then find an investor. You will flip the house to a flipper. The flipper will pay for the property, as well as give you a wholesaler's fee. You will make money without investing your own. This will get you in the game without taking any risks until you are ready to branch out on your own.

Scouting

This is similar to the wholesaling strategy. A scout will seek out a property and then match it with the investor without having to spend money at all. However, instead of selling the contract to an investor, the scout will sell this information about properties.

While this certain strategy does not generate a lot of profit as the other strategies, it does not have any risk involved. There is not much work that you have to do either. This means that a scout will sell the information much faster than the wholesaler.

Short Sales

This deals with foreclosure. A short sale is the very first of the three types. This will happen before a home is foreclosed on. Once a homeowner is not able to pay their mortgage, they will sell their home to an investor for less than they owe their lender. If the lender agrees on this, the lender will then accept cash and also forgive the rest of their loan.

There are benefits to both the seller as well as you. The seller will not have to deal with a foreclosure, and they will be able to save their credit. The flipper will be able to sell the house much cheaper than it should have been.

Foreclosures

The second option is purchasing a foreclosure. You will need to look for a foreclosure auction where you can bid on a home against other flippers or investors. A major drawback to this is the fact that you will not be able to look or inspect the property before you buy it. While this is a risky move, you can purchase these properties at a very low price in comparison to the typical house.

REOs

An REO is also known as real estate owned. This term is used to describe a property that is held by the lender; most times it is a bank, government loan insurer, or a government agency once the home is foreclosed. It will be sold for the outstanding loan amount. There is much less risk with the REOs over the standard foreclosure due to being able to look at the property before you buy it.

Chapter 8: Common Mistakes to Avoid

There are common mistakes that a lot of flippers make, and it will directly impact your profits. In this chapter, you will find out about common mistakes that flippers make when they are running their business. This ensures that you do not make the same errors to keep your properties from selling and prevents you from cutting into your profits. If you flip the home correctly, you should make anywhere from $25,000 up to $50,000 in profit. Here is the list of mistakes:

Not Having Experts for a Team

The team that you have for flipping should include a real estate agent, an inspector, an appraiser, a closing attorney or a title agent, a team of contractors, and a loan officer. This team is needed, and all of them have unique roles to play when you are flipping homes.

Flipping with the Wrong Price Range

While you can make money by flipping the low-end homes, you should research the homes around the one purchased to ensure you are selling it for a fair price, or you may not sell it at all.

Flipping in a Bad Location

There are specific markets that are much hotter than the others. A market that is hot is one that includes a high demand for renovated homes. Based on the gross profit margin, there are sites that find the best cities offering good areas to flip in. You will need to do some legwork to find the closest hot market in your vicinity. To get you jump-started here is a list of the top 10 cities and metro areas that offer high profits for flippers.

- Atlanta, Sandy Springs, Marietta – GA
- Chicago, Naperville, Joliet – IL
- Chattanooga – GA
- Richmond – VA
- York, Hanover – PA
- Deltona, Daytona Beach, Ormond Beach – FL
- Virginia Beach, Norfolk, Newport News – VA, NC
- Baltimore, Towson – MD
- New Orleans, Metairie, Kenner – LA
- Pittsburgh - PA

Here are the worst areas to flip in.

- San Francisco, Oakland, Fremont – CA
- Las Vegas, Paradise – NV
- Mobile – AL
- Charlotte, Gastonia, Concord – NC, SC
- Madison – WI
- Phoenix, Mesa, Scottsdale – AZ

- Houston, Sugar Land, Baytown – TX
- Oxnard, Thousand Oaks, Ventura – CA
- Fort Collins, Loveland – Co
  - Prescott – AZ

Not Having a Good Buy Formula

There is profit to be made when once there is money left over after you have subtracted all of your costs from the sale price. It will look like this:

- Add the Sale Price
- Minus the Purchase of the home.
- Minus the cost of the renovations.
- Minus the carrying costs like property taxes, insurance, utilities, etc.
- Minus the financing costs.
- Minus the closing costs like real estate commissions, title insurance, etc.
- This equals your profit.

Miscalculating Cost of Repairs

Real Estate Investing

Estimating the repairs is one of the crucial challenges of flipping a house. It is advised to double the projected budget, as well as the flipping timeline. This will give you much needed wiggle room to ensure that you do not fail on the flip. This cushion will make sure that you will make a profit and not waste time as well. Here is a condensed, quick list of what you will need to do to a home to flip it.

- *Exterior:*

o Tree limbs and shrubs.

o Mow the lawn

o Replace any dying bushes, plant some flowers, and get rid of anything dead.

o Apply a fresh layer of mulch.

o Remove any eyesores and clutter.

o Fill the driveway and the walkway cracks.

o Power was the house and put on fresh paint where there should be.

- o Replace or repair the screens and the windows.

- o Add or replace any shutters.

- o Paint the trim and front door.

- o Paint the garage to ensure that the house and garage matches.

- o Replace the home's gutters. Seamless gutters are the best. Make sure to install the splash blocks or gutter extensions.

- o Replace the rear and front storm doors.

- o Replace the outside light fixtures.

- o Replace the home's mailbox. Pick a design and color that will fit the neighborhood.

- Interior:

- o Give the home a good cleaning.

- o Wash all of the windows.

- o Install the new window blinds.

- Clean or replace drapes or the curtains.
- Remove the hooks and the nails from all of the walls and patch up the holes.
- Apply new paint to all of the rooms. Make sure to use flat and neutral colors.
- Check and repair all of the doors and the doorknobs. Doors should be able to open and close with little effort.
- Install new outlet covers and light switches.
- Install new smoke detectors.
- Replace the doorbell and the thermostat.
- Re-carpet, replace, or refinish the flooring.
- Swap out all of the register covers.
- Replace the exhaust fan covers and the fans.

- Kitchen:

- Install a new sink.
- Install a new faucet.

- o Refinish or replace the countertops and cabinets.

- o Apply new shelf liners to all of the drawers and shelves.

- Bathroom:

- o Install a new and updated vanity.

- o Install new fixtures.

- o Get a new toilet seat.

- o Get a new towel hanger.

- o Replace the shower curtain or get a glass shower door.

- o Apply new caulk around the shower and tub.

- o Scrub out the grout between the tiles.

- Bedrooms:

- o Paint the walls.

- o Re-carpet them.

- o Replace the light fixtures; register covers, and the cover plates.
- o Install the closet organizers if there are any.
- Basement:
- o Sweep away cobwebs.
- o Dust off the ductwork, wiring, and pipes.
- o Tack up any dangling cables.
- o Seal the cracks in the walls.
- o Whitewash the concrete and the cement block walls with some sealing paint.
- o Paint the floor with gray enamel.
- o Install some new glass block windows if it is needed.

Cheap House Syndrome

The cheapest home on the market is not always the best of deals. Do not be seduced by the most inexpensive property that you find. Most times a cheap house means that there is a lot to fix before you can sell it. This means that you will not make much profit or any profit at all due to all of the repairs that you will have to make.

Unrealistic Sale Prices

You will need to check the sale prices of the homes around the property that you are flipping. If you overprice the property, then you will not unload the flipping home. It will sit on the market for a long time and tie up the money. If you price the property appropriately, then you should be getting 3 to 4 showings a week on the one property. If you do not get that many viewings in a week, you should consider dropping your price down in $5,000 increments.

Not Adding in Enough Value

As a market softens up, the successful flippers will need to focus on finding some properties where they can add value. If they do not add enough value, then the house will not produce enough profits for the flipper.

Ignoring Curb Appeal

The exterior offers the first impression of a home to the buyers. The interior will be impeccable; however, if the outside does not draw in the buyers, then they will not even see the inside and it will not have an impact. For example, if you flip a house that has a cracked driveway, then people will automatically think the inside reflects problems. They will not give the home a chance. It is important to put a little extra time and effort into the small things that will add to the home's curb appeal.

Holding Out for the Best Offer

Time is an enemy of the flipper. The longer a home sits on the market waiting for a potential buyer, the lower the price will need to go. Do not hold out too long for a better offer, for that offer shall never come. You will lose out on the profits that you could have had before greed set in. You should hold out for a good offer, but not too long.

Thinking that You Will Become Rich Fast

Do not forget that flipping does have risks involved. Plan on learning everything you can. You will pay the price for your success. Not all of the deals will be a good one. Even after you have done hundreds of flips, you will still have an agreement that is not a winner. Do not enter into a flipping business unless you have a long-term type of perspective.

Not Having a Large Enough Profit Margin

Many investors will go into a deal with thin margins. Anything that is less than 20 percent is too small of a profit margin. You will need to ensure that the margin is great enough so that you can get more significant gain within the rehab budget.

Not Understanding the Real Estate Market

It is important to comprehend the real estate market cycle. When it comes to investing in real estate, you will need to ensure that you are well aware of what the current cycle is. This aids in the business of flipping houses.

Doing All of the Work Yourself

Real Estate Investing

While you may be a handy flipper, you may need to hire professionals. It will add in the value that you are hoping to gain. The reality of it is that there are limits to the handiness that a person has. Not everyone is perfect in every aspect. You will need to know what your limits are and hire someone else to pick up where your weaknesses are. For example, if you find that the professionals are better at installing carpeting, then you should allow them to do it and you move on to the next project.

This chapter is going to breakdown the process of actually purchasing the property – from the offer to the inspection and all the way to the closing. Buying a fixer-upper is nearly the same process as buying your personal residence, but we want to share with you a couple of tricks of the trade that will protect you.

The Purchase Agreement

There are two basic types of properties that you will be purchasing – the properties that are listed with a licensed agent (in the MLS) and those that are not (FSBOs). For Sale by Owner (FSBO) properties can be a little more of a challenge because you do not have anyone in your corner advocating your rights. But basically the processes are the same. In fact, I recommend you use the same purchase agreement.

For your first couple of transactions, it is a good idea to work along with your real estate agent to find listed properties. Though the discounting may not be as great, the buying process carries less risk and your agent will help you become intimately familiar with the buying process.

Real estate agents have their own purchase agreements. Once you locate a property, they will fill out the form for you and submit it to the buyer's agent. If you decide to step out and make your own offers on non-listed properties, copy that same form and use it for your offers. Just remove statements that link the form to any real estate companies, agents or licensing authorities. Since these are state mandated forms, all the legal protection clauses are in there. No sense reinventing the wheel.

Purchase Price

As we have previously discussed, you will want to pay the lowest possible price, but in some markets, properties are selling at or even above the list price. In that case, it can be almost impossible to get a buyer to consider a discounted offer.

Do not give up, just change your strategy. You can always make a full price offer and then renegotiate for a lower price after your inspection reveals the costly problems with the property.

Safety Clauses

Purchase agreements always come with contingency clauses. There are some clauses that are particularly effective for property flippers.

- Subject to Inspection

This is a standard contingency for all purchase agreements – and it is even more so for fixer-upper properties. Though you realize that the home needs repair – hence the reason you are buying it – but there is a difference between renovating the kitchen and rebuilding the foundation. If after your full inspection you find that there are just too many repairs, this clause allows you to negotiate a new purchase price or simply back out of the offer.

• Subject to Financing

If you are getting financing, you should be pre-approved before submitting an offer, but if for some reason you are suddenly denied the loan, this clause is your ticket out of the agreement.

• Subject to Appraisal

If your offer is substantially below what you believe to be the market value, this clause is not necessary. But if you believe you can do a quick flip, you will want to make doubly sure that you are not paying too much.

The fewer contingencies that you have in a purchase agreement, the more likely it is to be accepted. Sellers generally scorn offers that require them to pay the buyer's closing costs. They also rarely accept offers that are contingent on the sale of another property.

Earnest Money Deposits

You can expect to pay some sort of earnest money deposit to prove to the seller that you are a serious buyer. These deposits are always held by a third party and are not released to the seller until closing. The deposit will be applied to the purchase price.

Make sure that your purchase agreement states that the EMD will be paid after the seller's acceptance. If you are writing a lot of offers, you do not want to wrap up thousands of dollars on offers that go nowhere.

The Inspection

The inspection is no doubt the most important part of the purchase process. Of course, before you submit an offer, you are going to want to take your time and inspect the property. Once the offer is accepted, this is where you inspect the property with a fine toothcomb. This leads to being able to prepare an accurate estimate of the renovation work.

Who to Bring

Unless you have a builder's license and years of on-the-job experience as a contractor, I highly recommend that you bring your general contractor with you. Even if you have to pay him for his time, it will be worth every penny. He will no doubt find issues that you may have missed. He will also be able to identify load-bearing walls.

You could also hire a home inspector. These inspection professionals will cost between $400 and $600. Unlike your contractor, he or she will be looking for issues that affect either the safety or security of the home. This would include mold identification, infestations, electrical issues, code violations, plumbing problems etc.

Bringing your agent along with you is also a good idea. As your contractor makes suggestions on how to improve the property, your agent will be able to gauge the market's response and how it will affect the market value.

What to Bring

There are a few standard items you will want to bring to an inspection... and a few unusual items. Your contractor will no doubt bring them as well, but better to have two of something than none at all. Here is a list of what I recommend:

Camera:

This is a great way to document problems. It also serves as a good memory aid.

Measuring Tape:

Yeah, I know you already have one in your glove compartment.

Flashlight:

Comes in handy in the crawl spaces, attics and dark corners in the cabinets.

Construction Level:

"Is that wall really plumb? Something in that railing just doesn't line up. Hand me the level, please."

Binoculars:

You could climb up on the roof to inspect the shingles, or you could stand on solid ground and use your binoculars.

Marble:

There is no quicker way to see if a floor is level or if the kitchen cabinets were hung straight.

Where to Look

When inspecting a property for the first time, walk through the whole house to get a feel for it. Then start on one floor and slowly go through each room, each closet, each nook and cranny. Write down everything that is out of the ordinary. Take a picture of all of it.

Your inspection needs to cover three basic areas:

🏠

Layout

– Remember that buyers want an open floor plan. There should be a nice flow of the house – or the potential to create one. You do not want to have to pass through a bedroom to reach another area of the house.

Condition

– Look at the carpet, the tile, the paint, and the trim. Carefully inspect the electrical, plumbing and heating systems. These can be real expensive items to replace and unfortunately buyers want them but don't especially like to pay you back for fixing them.

Potential

– The real money lies in converting an ugly house into a beauty. You need to look behind the hideous carpet, the repulsive paint colors and the completely dated kitchen and envision what you could do with the place. In fact, the uglier the house, the greater the potential to make an easy buck.

When to Run Away

Okay, so we are looking for unappealing, unattractive ugly houses to work our magic on but there are some properties that just are not worth the effort. There are properties that should make you turn tail and run away – well after you invoke your inspection contingency.

Mold -

 Mold remediation can be very expensive. If a buyer learns there was a serious mold problem it can be a big turn off. If it is just one small spot, be prepared to replace the drywall or flooring in that area. If, however, there is mold in the walls - RUN!

Termites

- If you or your inspector suspects an infestation, you should hire a pest control specialists to see how severe it is. Surface termite damage is one thing, but if you find that they have or are attacking structural components – RUN!

Foundation Problems.

There is no money in jacking up a house and replacing the whole foundation. Buyers want a level foundation but don't expect them to pay for it. Foundation problems can cause on going issues for the whole house – even after it is fixed. The best idea is just to stay away and leave it to the professionals.

Environmental Problems.

The last thing you want is to buy a property that has land contamination. The United States Environmental Protection Agency (EPA) has an interactive website to check for reported contamination.

If after the inspection you find some surprises that are not in your budget, do not think that they are automatically a deal breaker. If you are working with a highly motivated seller with a "handyman special," they may be ready to fix the problem themselves, adjust the purchase price or credit the cost. If you want to reduce paying income taxes, have them credit the cost rather than lower the price.

At this point we are going to jump into the deep end and show you how to make money-flipping properties. We are going to start with the easiest and quickest – the Quick Flip.

Properties that are Good for a Quick Flip

If you want to make money off a quick flip, then you have to find properties at a cheap price. Real estate agents are going to price the properties at market value so it can be a challenge to find super cheap properties in the MLS. Here are a few other suggestions:

Real Estate Investing

For Sale by Owner

Highly Motivated Sellers

- Job Transfers

- Retiring Landlords

- Pre-Foreclosures

Transitional Properties

Ugly Properties

What is a Quick Flip?

> These are properties that require few re-pairs and no rehabs.

> The key is to purchase these properties at a substantial discount.

Change the Look for Cheap

Properties that are superficially ugly have a great potential to earn a quick dollar in exchange for a bottle of bleach and a couple of gallons of paint. If you want to change the look of a house for cheap consider:

- **A Fresh Coat of Paint.**

  Stick to neutral modern colors.

- **Replace the Fixtures.**

  Exchange brass for silver, globe lights for ceiling fans and upgrade fixtures to a more modern design.

- **New Hardware.**

  It is amazing how the look of a house changes with new knobs, pulls, switches and even hinges.

- **Landscaping.**

Aim for low maintenance. A few well-placed shrubs and some hardy flowers can do wonders. Lighting also creates a great first impression.

A Bright Front Door.

For some reason, buyers love a brightly colored front door. Spray paint it, don't use a brush.

Change the Backyard.

Create a backyard that is safe for the kids and is easy to entertain in.

How to Make Money Flipping Without a Rehab

In order to maximize your return, here are a few tips that can help you:

Always buy below market

Surface changes do not change value, they change perception. An appraiser is going to look past the new faucets and the pretty front door and look at the structure and the market – but your buyers are not nearly that objective. You want to buy the property below market and then sell it at the top of the market value.

Reduce your holding period

The quicker you can resell the property, the less holding costs you will pay (less mortgage interest, taxes, insurance, utilities etc.). If you want to really profit off of it, sell it yourself and save yourself the commission. Start advertising for a buyer as soon as you have waived your purchase contingencies. You could even let your buyers pick out the paint colors.

If you really want to keep it easy, find a buyer before you even close on your purchase. If is a non-bank REO, put "and assigns" after your name on the purchase agreement and then simply assign the contract to your new buyers. You get a check for the difference between your purchase price and the sales price to your end buyer – and your end buyer pays the closing costs.

Another option is to do a double close. You close with the seller (the A/B transaction) and then immediately close with your end buyer (the B/C transaction). The funds from the B/C transaction are used to pay off the A/B. Not all title companies are willing to take the risk of floating the A/B transaction. If you can get your end buyer to escrow his funds with the title company before the A/B transaction, then the liability is reduced.

When trying to sell a property yourself, you need to keep every lead you ever find – whether they are interested right now or not. Who knows, they might not like this property but how about the one you are working on 6 months from now.

Most of your properties are going to be in this category. They will need varying degrees of repairs, renovation or rehabs to maximize their resale value. The renovation takes much more planning and skill, but it can generate a great deal of satisfaction – and money.

How to Find the Property

While there are properties that could benefit from a rehab all over the place, some properties lend themselves to this more than others. Focus your attention on:

- Fixer-Uppers

- Transitional Properties

- Abandoned Homes

- Stalled Construction

- Multi-family Conversion

Real Estate Investing

- Auction Properties

- Divorce

- Estate Sales

What's the Difference?

> *Repairs:* To restore the property to a good condition.

> *Renovation:* To make the property new or as if new again. To reinvigorate, refresh or revive.

> *Rehabilitation:* To make livable or to restore to

How to Determine Profitability

This is where you are going to need a calculator. Profitability is a combination of purchase price, holding costs, accurate renovation estimates and your desired profit. Here is the formula again as a reminder:

(ARV x .70) - Rehab Costs = Maximum Allowable Offer

The Purchase Price

It all starts with the purchase price. If you "accidentally" over pay by 5 to 10% then you are going to have that same amount cut out of your profit when you sell. So, how do you know if you are buying a property for a fair price? Your network is invaluable. It is not just a matter of getting a CMA from your agent but also consulting with your contractor. Sure, the property is worth $185,000 until you find out the roof needs a total replacement.

The Rehab

If you think the price you pay for the property is important, the work estimates can make or break your project. Renovation never goes as smooth as you hope. If you want to play it safe, get your written (remember written) estimates and then add 5% to them. If you can do it for less, great more profit for you! But if things get complicated, you have a cushion.

There are some projects that are vastly more profitable than others. Here are the top 5 renovations in order of demand:

Kitchen:

Don't think you have to drop $25K - $50,000 to renovate a kitchen. Resurfacing cabinets keeps the structure (which is usually still good) while giving them an updated and more modern face (which is usually the problem). Consider concrete countertops manufactured to look like granite (for a fraction of the cost and all the durability).

Baths:

New flooring, fresh colors and new fixtures can change drab to chic. His and her sinks in the master bathroom are a good seller. Look to tuck a powder room in on the main floor.

Open Floor Plan:

Older homes are great fixer-uppers but they tend to be choppy and claustrophobic. Removing a non-load bearing wall to open up the living area can move a 1950's house up into the 21st century.

Landscaping and Curb Appeal:

First impressions are important. Keep the yard green and well trimmed. Clean the siding and the gutters. Paint the front door. Replace the garage door if needed and add some shrubs and flowers.

Flooring:

Old ratty flooring really dates a house. Don't just slam something down and call it new. Moving up from vinyl to tile and carpet to wood can move a house up to a new price level if done tastefully.

Other Projects:

Other options that buyers are willing to pay for include additional bedrooms and baths along with garage and attic conversions. Master suite additions can dramatically increase the resale value but often do not return the full amount so work closely with your contractor, appraiser and agent.

The After Repair Value

At this point, don't take a shot in the dark. Talk to your contractor about what he recommends and get the estimates in writing. Now take these estimates to your real estate agent. You need to know if spending $15,000 on the kitchen is going pay you back the $15,000 and at least earn you your 20% or $3,000. Your agent will need to do a CMA on the finished product to determine your After Repair Value (AVR).

When you get your ARV, this number is now gospel. The ARV cannot be tweaked, edged up, altered or adjusted. When you start saying, "Oh don't worry, I'll just ask $5,000 more – we'll get it, I'm sure. Because…" you are treading on very thin ice. This is the number one reason property flippers fail – they keep changing the ARV on the property. Don't do it. Change your repairs. Change your profit margin. But do not change the ARV. Trust your agent.

Do It Yourself vs. Hiring a Contractor

Sure, you've done all sorts of repairs around your house. You even upgraded your own kitchen. You've got 'skilz'. Unfortunately, just because you know how to use a circular saw and to swing a hammer does not mean that you are an experienced renovation expert. There is a big difference from fixing your own house and remodeling a home you intend to market. We tend to overlook little mistakes but buyer and especially inspectors will not.

Buyers are going to bring through their home inspector. A botched job could cost you the deal and actually lower the price. You also need to consider that some work requires a license and/or permits. In that case, doing the work yourself is definitely not recommended.

Use your contractor for detail specific work where accuracy and perfection are important. Save the "grunt" work for yourself if you are so inclined. There are some other considerations beside your experience and abilities:

- Do you still have a full-time job?

- Do you really want to spend every weekend for 6 months with a hammer, chisel and paint brush?

Can you afford the repairs if you quit your job and focus on this project?

Contractors are used to working on a deadline, whereas as homeowners commonly tend to procrastinate and put off what they can do tomorrow. Every week that passes is another week that you have to pay holding costs. The quicker you can turn the project over, the quicker you will make your profit. Perhaps you may want to consider leaving the construction to your contractor and become the general manager instead.

How to Manage the Rehab

Time is money. Ensuring that all your contractors are getting the work done on schedule will pay off in the end. It take 'skilz' to schedule all the different contractors and jobs to maximize the time.

There will also be bills to be paid and a budget to scrutinize. You need to keep your contractors and your desire to keep upgrading reigned in on the budget. The minute you exceed market tolerances by upgrading or overbuilding, you are cutting into your profit margin.

Stay organized by creating to-do lists. As you get close to completing the project, create a final punch list of all the little things that perhaps the contractor "over looked."

Chapter 9: Transitional Properties

Transitional properties are perhaps one of the most overlooked gold mines for property flippers. As humans, we resist change. Our eyes dictate utility. We miss opportunities.

For example, an area was recently rezoned from residential to office/service. There is a high traffic road that runs through this new-zoned area. On that road are several older residential homes.

One was listed for sale. The asking price is $185,000. It is old and in need of some serious attention but after a little research you find out that the lot itself is worth $75,000. So the value is in the land. Land typically represents 20% of the property value. That means this site could feasibly carry a price of $375,000 if a brand new office building was built on it.

What is a Transitional Property?

A property that is on the verge of being transformed into a new utility such as a residential home that was rezoned for office use.

But what about that old house? It is now a transitional property. The value is no longer in its utility as a residential property but in its conversion into an office building.

All you need to do is to change the market perception of the home and change it into a professional office. Take out the features that make this a "home" and create an office atmosphere with a reception area, lunchroom and offices. Attorneys, tax consultants, insurance salesmen and real estate companies often buy these types of properties.

Where to Start

Keep track of your local planning and zoning office. Follow their activity. Go to their public meetings. Where are they changing the zoning? Where are areas of new construction? Where are the changes?

Legal Considerations

Transitional properties are often grandfathered in or are considered legally non-conforming. That means that a residential home though under the office zoning does not need to meet the building requirements for a new office building. But… if you start renovating a property, that could all change. So, before you jump in, make sure that you know what you are getting into and what will be required if you alter the utility of the building.

To Renovate or Not to Renovate?

Not all buildings will lend themselves to being renovated. In that case, you may consider buying an appropriately zone lot and moving the structure.

Take the above example, if all the surrounding construction is of a modern strip mall type, having a house in the middle may not have much appeal. Why not buy a residential lot and move the house. The vacant commercial land could be sold for $75,000 and you have a house that could be renovated and sold for full price as well.

Another option is one of simple marketing. FSBO sellers rarely consider transitional value. Grandma and Grandpa have lived here for 55 years but they can't stand the traffic anymore. They want out. They never in a million years thought that the land they paid $2,500 for 55 years ago would be worth $75,000. They only think of it as a home. You pick up the property for $110,000 and immediately turn around and sell it to another rehabber for $150,000 and pocket $40,000 tomorrow.

Chapter 10: How to Sell the Finished Product

While you are upgrading and renovating the property, you only have money going out. Now it is time to get some money coming in. The time has come to reap the rewards from all your hard work.

Selling With an Agent vs. Selling On Your Own

Buying a property with the help of your real estate agent is a no-brainer. Since the seller pays their commission, their services are free to you. When it comes to selling, however, their services, experience and assistance will cost you quite a bit.

Paying commission is a significant expense to factor into your profitability equation. When you multiplied your ARV by .70, the commission is automatically figured in as part of your 30% profit margin. Typically real estate agents will charge 5-7% of the sales price. On a $250,000 sale, you are looking between $12,500 and $17,500. If you have a good real estate agent, however, it is totally worth it.

Your agent will do more than simply find you a buyer. They foot the cost for the marketing of your property. They take the time to show all interested parties the home. They will negotiate with buyers and their agents to get you the highest price possible. They will work with the agency that is handling the closing to make sure everything is completed. If there are any complications in any of these areas, your agent will step up to the plate and work to resolve them.

This frees up your time to focus on finding your next investment. You need to weigh whether you have the resources and the skills necessary to take their place if you decide to go it alone. Real estate transactions are rarely cut and dried, the potential for a lawsuit from a dissatisfied buyer is always present. Having a licensed agent is a prime way to reduce the likelihood of that happening.

That being said, I would recommend that for your first couple of properties, you use the services of an agent. It will help prepare you for the realities of selling the property, if you decide to go at it alone down the road.

How to Attract Buyers

The quicker you can locate the buyer the better. You want them to pick your home over the others that are competing against you. Here are some suggestions that will make your property stand out above the crowd.

Staging

Buyers need a little encouragement to envision how the home will look when furnished. Empty rooms do little to spur imagination.

It has been proven that a home, which has been well, staged sells for more than if the home was sold vacant – even though the buyer keeps none of the furnishings.

You have three basic options: Professional stagers, rent-to-own companies and the do-it-yourself option. Professional stagers are worth the cost if you are selling a mid-to-high range home. Another option is to rent a living room and master bedroom set from a rental company and then return it when the house sells. If you need to reduce costs and are looking for the minimum, put up some neutral curtains and set out some healthy houseplants.

Open Houses

Having an open house is a great way to show the community what you have done to improve the property. Display before and after photos. Make sure you set out some flyers and business cards. You just may get a good referral out of it.

Lease Options and Land Contracts

Quite a few buyers have decent credit but lack the down payment necessary to get a loan. If after a though background check and credit report, you deem them to be low risk, consider selling the home on a lease option or land contract. Though this will lock up your capital for a year or two, the additional payments and interest can increase your return. The lease option will entail two documents – one for the lease and the other for the purchase. The renter will pay market rent plus a monthly payment for the future purchase of the house. If they back out of the lease option, all payments are non-refundable.

Another option is to sell the property on a land contract. The down payment is less (generally less than 10%) but the interest rate is higher than conventional loans. After three to five years, the buyer must pay off the loan freeing up your capital.

Chapter 11: Challenges to Property Flipping

Property flipping is a very profitable business for those who are willing to work hard, stick to a budget and invest in the right properties. There are, however, some challenges that can make this business a risky and often stressful one. Here are the top five challenges and how to get around them:

1. Flipping is not always profitable.

It is very difficult to make money-flipping properties when price appreciation slows or reverses. Property flippers expect property values to have increased during the holding period, which adds to their bottom line.

In strong markets, a lack of discounted homes and foreclosure deals can reduce the supply and increase competition among flippers. Property flipping in higher-priced markets such as San Francisco, Seattle, Denver, New York City and Los Angeles can be a real challenge since it costs so much to get the property in the first place.

Flippers who do this full-time often run into cash flow problems. While the property is under construction, it is constant money going out. It can take six months of renovation bills in order to see any income. Flippers need to stay on top of the market and have a reasonable plan to pay for the repairs.

2. Lack of Experience

Poor quality renovations and repairs can actually pull down the value of the home as buyers see it more as a liability than an upgrade. Make sure you use your contractor where it counts, it will be worth the money spent.

3. Lengthy Holding Period

Flippers who drag their feet during the renovation period will see rising holding costs, which will slowly eat away at their profits. In addition, there are periods during the year where buyers are few and far between. Time your construction to fall during the slow times such as November – February and then put the home on the market as buyers come out of hibernation.

4. Tax Implications

Because you will sell the property within the first year of ownership, you will not have to pay capital gains tax, but the profit you make off the sale will be taxed as ordinary income. Unless your tax advisor or accountant helps you to set up the appropriate corporation, it will be taxed as self-employment income. When it comes to corporations, look into an S-Corp rather than a LLC. S-Corps offer more tax advantages and legal protections than LLCs. So, before you go out and spend all your profits, make sure you set aside around 25% to pay your taxes… and make an appointment to consult with your CPA.

5. The ARV is Constantly Changing

More than any other challenge, this one here causes the death of a property flipper more than any other. Flippers who always think they can sell the property for a little more will quickly find out that the market is not that gullible. Get a reliable ARV and stick to it, no matter what.

Chapter 12: 10 Tips to Make the Most Money Flipping Houses

Would you like to know a few of the trade secrets? Well I am going to let you in on a few tips I have picked up over the years. Implementing these points will reduce risk and stress and increase profits.

1. Do not take on more risk than you can bear.

2. Choose the best investment, not the first property.

3. Correctly calculate your holding costs.

4. Do not overbuild.

5. Do not run out of money and stall the project.

6. Watch your time vs. money. If it takes you 6 months of working full-time on the rehab to make $5,000 profit, you are only earning $5.20 an hour.

7. Be patient. Professionals take their time and wait for the right property. Novices rush out and buy the first fixer-upper they find and hire the cheapest contractor.

8. Try to sell the house yourself and save the commission.

9. Develop a system. Create a step-by-step process. Use the same suppliers, the same materials, the same paint colors and the same timeline where possible. Not only will it simplify the process and reduce stress but also it will make it much easier to estimate renovation costs.

10. Always estimate more for repairs than what you think. Repairs frequently cost more than estimated and unforeseen repairs always show up, so be prepared from the start.

And... If you really want to maximize your return, consider living in the property while renovating. In this way you are always on-site and can work longer and harder on a project. Meanwhile, your holding costs are your living expenses. While this may work well for singles, I do not recommend it for newlyweds or families with children – for obvious reasons.

Real Estate Investing

How to Get Started

I hope this book has helped you to understand the ins and outs of property flipping. If you dream of working for yourself and enjoy working with your hands and have the skills to boot, this can be a truly rewarding line of work – and a profitable one at that.

Now it comes to the point getting it off the paper and into reality. If you are ready to get started, here is where you should begin:

1. Figure out your financing.

    a. Save for a down payment.

    b. Get pre-approved.

    c. Figure out how to pay for the repairs.

2. Partner with a real estate agent.

3. Find a contractor.

4. Find 20 houses.

    a. MLS

    b. Notice of Defaults

    c. Non-listed run down properties

    d. FSBOs

5. Analyze them all.

    a. Analyze the property

    b. Study the market

    c. Determine buyer's wants and needs.

6. Make an offer on the best options.

7. After the closing, start the work.

    a. Stay on budget

    b. Watch your costs vs. ARV

    c. Do the highest quality work possible.

8. While in the end stages of construction, market the property.

9. Sell the property.

10. Repeat from Step 4.

It all starts with one good property. Once that is rehabbed and sold, the profits can be slid over into the next investment and then the business grows, the systems improve and the return on your investments compound. So just don't sit there, go for it!

Chapter 13: Financing Your Business

Conventional Financing Options

Although conventional financing is an option for real estate investments, for several reasons it is typically not the first type sought. By definition, conventional financing is any loan not eligible for federal insurance or guaranteed by a government agency. Examples of government agencies are Housing and Urban Development (HUD), Government National Mortgage Association (GNMA), Federal Housing Association (FHA), Veterans Administration (VA), and the Farmers Home Administration (FmHA).

The various programs are required to meet the guidelines of Fannie Mae or Freddie Mac and sometimes referred to as conforming loans. The most obvious guideline limitation is the maximum loan limit Fannie Mae and Freddie Mac and adjusted each year to account for the change in average home sales prices nationwide. Government-sponsored and monitored programs typically have a required laundry list of criteria before financing can be approved. As with most government-managed processes, securing financing for one of these programs often takes longer than conventional loans approved only by the bank providing the financing.

Many types of conventional loan programs are available. The programs include fixed rate, adjustable rate (ARM), balloon, biweekly, and convertible. In addition to the types of conventional loans, loan programs also offer a variety of approval criteria and features. The terms, loan-to-value, varying income, no-income-verification, and various credit score requirements, are just a few variables given different levels of consideration to achieve the desired outcome. In other words, loan officers have more to work with in conventional lending situations when seeking approval and to sell you or your business on your behalf.

Real estate investment loans are not always considered conventional. As a result, you are not given the same terms as someone buying the home to reside in. Buying investment property for rental purposes, or to renovate and sell again, is considered a commercial investment and commercial loan terms apply. Many of the residential loan approval criteria are also applicable for commercial loan approval and consideration as well.

Much like residential mortgage loans, different banks offer programs and packages for their commercial lenders. Always do your homework before you accept loan terms from any one institution. Ask about the difference between conventional residential and commercial. Ask about programs specific to your type of business. If you ask enough of the right questions, banks may then begin to offer more information than they otherwise would have. Most loan officers are paid in a salary-plus commission structure. They want to secure financing for you, however, they may also be motivated to sell you loan programs that offer them a higher commission. So, be sure to ask enough of the right questions so they present all of the options.

Ultimately, the decision for loan approval comes from a higher power than the loan officer. The decision will come from either a local board or a corporate underwriting department. If you are working with an involved loan program, the decision for approval comes from the sponsoring government program.

Don't give out your Social Security Number or your business identification number to every loan officer you talk with. There is truth to the fact that every time a credit check is run against your Social Security Number it pulls your credit rating down.

Creative Financing Options "No money down," exclaimed the naysayer, "you can't do that. It's not ethical." Many people watch the "How to Buy Real Estate" infomercials on late night and weekend television and see slick productions and pitchmen promising riches beyond belief if only the viewer will use their credit card and call in. In fairness, there is some solid information being offered (sometimes, I watch them, too).

There is a lot of hype from folks who make their money selling expensive programs and boot camps. If you purchase their program, you have to have the tenacity and discipline to read the materials and follow their prescribed formula to make a go of it. But let's get to the real question: Can you really buy real estate with no money down? The answer is, yes!

People have been led to believe it's impossible to purchase property without using your own cash. However, I've been doing it successfully since the late 1970s when I was forced to simply to survive. Much of what I know is a direct result of the real estate depression (not a slow down or recession) in Bend, Oregon, which began at that time and ran through the mid-1980s.

Things were not pretty— but I learned a lot of valuable lessons during that time. I regularly purchase with little or no cash out of my pocket. In fact, at one time I closed a $5,500,000 real estate purchase without using my own money. In addition, I actually received a check at the end of closing. I almost never buy a house if I have to pay money out of pocket.

Perhaps the more important question is: Can you afford 100-percent financing and still enjoy cash flow? Even if you could secure a 100% loan, would that be a good idea? The answer is: Maybe, Maybe not. It depends on your strategy. At this point I will say that 100% financing may not be a good thing.

Here are some important questions for you to consider. I know I mentioned it earlier, but it is worth mentioning again. I teach my protégées to ask four questions when entering into a real estate purchase:

1. Does this purchase create wealth today?
2. How much money out of my pocket will this transaction take?
3. When do I get that money back?
4. Does this project have a positive cash flow?

If you have positive answers to these questions, you may have a good deal. Before you spend your hard-earned money for a dream of real estate riches, here is a list of ways to purchase with no money down.

Talk to Your Lender

One member of your success team should be a lender with whom you regularly do business. Call that team member and ask about zero down loan programs. There are now several options available to you—especially if you are a first time homebuyer.

There are also FHA and federal VA loans that are very close to zero down. It is possible to get an 80-percent loan-to-value first mortgage and a 20-percent second, but be careful. The monthly payments may be too expensive to justify the purchase. It is imperative you run an investment analysis for each property you consider for purchase. The truth is in the numbers, and your lender will be pleased to see that you get that, even before you talked to them. If you can prove through your analysis that it is a wise investment that will go a long way to achieving success in securing a loan.

Home Equity Line of Credit -- (HELOC)
At this writing HELOCS are a thing of the past. One thing I used to do was carry a Home Equity Line of Credit (called HELOC) on each rental I own. Then if cash is needed to close a deal I can write a check from the account. I had more than $600,000 in credit lines from my HELOC loans. One bank has given me a credit card tied to my HELOC with a credit line of $99,999.

You should, however, use caution when using a line of credit. The first thing I ask myself before drawing money from a HELOC is, when will I get this money back to pay off the loan? If you can't answer that question, do not borrow the money. Any cash advance will increase your monthly payments.

Also make sure you are not upside down with your cash flow. That is a common mistake of many new investors. The financial analysis you prepare before you purchase a property shouldn't be sweetened in any way to make the deal look better on paper than it really is. If you can't achieve cash flow or a reasonable return on your investment, find a different property.

Seller Financing

Don't overlook the possibility of the seller lending you the down payment. If you are marketing and talking to the right sellers – specifically motivated ones, they may well help you get your first mortgage by loaning you enough money to close the deal. I frequently use that technique.

I have had a seller loan me as much as $500,000 with no interest for the first 6 months. I then made sure I turned the property over before 6 months. By the way, the $500,000 could just as easily be $1,000,000 on the right deal. If the seller has a lot of equity or is in foreclosure, creative options are available.

Raise the Price and Lower the Terms

If you offer the seller more than he is asking, you may be able to pull this one off. He has to be willing to accept the down payment in the form of a note if the house appraises well enough to justify the price increase.

For example, a seller is asking $250,000 for his house with a $15,000 down payment and he is willing to carry the balance of $235,000. You offer him $255,000, or more, in the form of a promissory note instead of cash. He gets a little more return for the extra risk involved. Use your imagination. That's the only thing that restricts your success.

Use Your Investment Property Inventory
On occasion, I borrowed against another property I own. I currently have a note and trust deed on an investment property that I used instead of cash. That meant I didn't have to come up with dollars to close the deal and gives me tremendous flexibility. Imagine what is possible if you don't always have to borrow the money for your down payment.

Find an Investor
One trick I teach my protégées is to search for successful people who want to be real estate investors but do not have the time to spend on research. They have the cash and financial strength

to do a deal so you help out by supplying the time it takes to locate and negotiate the purchase.

I have several protégées who are in a position to make $100,000 to $500,000 each year without using their cash or credit. They will not do a deal unless there is at least $30,000 total profit in the transaction. Their share in that size of profit is $15,000. This is a great way to get started as an investor. You provide the work and expertise and let your partner supply the money and credit.

Use Your Commission

If you are a real estate broker/agent, use your commission to get what you want. I use mine when I purchase real estate such as single-family homes, duplexes, bare land, or subdivisions. On one transaction alone I made $350,000 this year. The seller told me what price he wanted, and I added my commission to it.

On single-family homes, using your own commission works well when you are dealing with a For Sale by Owner (FSBO). I have added to their asking price a fee of 3 percent for closing costs and 7 percent for a sales commission I then used on the down payment. Again, be creative.

Lease Option

If you have never done a lease option, also called to as a Rent-To-Own, you owe it to yourself to start. There are several great reasons to lease option. Some argue that it's best to control rather than own. This is especially true if you have poor credit and you can't, or won't, find a financial partner.

You can negotiate leases with landlords who want to stop being a landlord or an owner and who can't sell a house. Negotiate a small down payment ($100?) but be sure that the payment, or a portion of it, is deducted from the sales price. You should maintain the right to sublease. If possible, make sure your monthly payment is below current rents, then offer to sell the property on a lease option at a higher price than you negotiated, with $5,000 down in the form of option consideration. Then charge an extra $100 to $200 per month in order for you to realize positive cash flow.

Trade for It

Another technique is to offer the seller something they might need or want. Cash is not the only form of payment. I have traded many times for down payments. Possibilities include such things as boats, cars, recreational vehicles, tractors, gemstones, silver or gold, or personal services. Discover what the seller really wants and offer it for trade.

Your Family and Friends

You may be able to borrow the money you need from your family, friends, or business partner, but I urge you to be fair and honest with them. Many friendships and family relationships have been strained or lost because of a bad business deal. You may want to offer them a portion of the profit when the property is sold. If they are willing to loan you money, nurture the relationship so you will have the opportunity to borrow again if needed.

If you learn to invest in real estate without using your own hard-earned cash, you will realize returns that can exceed 1,000 percent at a time when many think a 10 percent or 50 percent return is good. If you have money in the bank, I have a challenge for you; on your next real estate transaction, think outside the box and do not use any of your own money. It will open up a whole new world for you.

Your Credit Rating

I now want to turn your attention to credit. There are many real estate gurus who tell us we don't need good credit to make millions of dollars in the real estate market. While that is certainly true, and I have shown many investors how that can be done, with good credit you can make much more.

Poor credit is a weight around your neck that can kill many good deals. It limits your alternatives and options when the money market dries up. Besides, it is a reflection of your character. A person who isn't faithful paying their monthly bills is a person whose word is not very believable.

The person with "challenged" credit, as we sometimes generously say, has a flashing neon sign on his back that declares: "I know I promised to pay, and I had good intentions, but I decided to buy a new car and take my wife to dinner instead."

Here is what I suggest:

1. Run a credit report and make a list of your debts. This will identify whom you have to pay and when you should pay.

2. Don't roll your debt into a credit card and then another. While this may seem like the answer to your problem, you are only creating a larger monster to deal with later.

3. Prioritize your credit list. When facing our financial problems, my wife and I had to work hard to get back to square one. We took the following:

   a. We listed our creditors and chose to pay off the ones with the least amount of balance while making minimum payments to the others.
   b. When the first debt was paid off, we took the amount we were paying and applied it to the next one on the list.

    c. We repeated the process until we were paying large amounts each month to the final credit card.

    d. We changed our lifestyle. We rarely ate out; we drove used cars and took low-cost family vacations only if we could do it without using our credit card. My wife shopped for bargains and clipped vendor coupons. It was difficult but well worth it to get back on our feet.

4. Use credit cards sparingly, keep low balances and pay on time. Some writers advise us to destroy our credit cards once they are paid in full. I think it's better to keep them and use them carefully to show the credit reporting agencies that you use credit wisely. In that way you can rebuild your credit rating, making available more options to fund your real estate purchases.

5. Establish a realistic monthly budget and stick to it. It's the only way to get out of debt and rehabilitate your credit.

6. Be extremely careful with the equity in your home. You don't want to draw out your equity and pay off your debt if you have not cured the problem. I've seen many people get into debt, refinance their home (or get a Home Equity Line of Credit), and spend their equity while not addressing the real issue of uncontrollable spending.

7. There are many resources available to help you overcome your indebtedness so use them. It has been said, "The more you learn, the more you earn." That is true with regard to building a good credit rating. Use these basic steps to start immediately paying down your debts. You will have many more nights of sound sleep knowing that the phone is not going to ring with a collector at the other end wanting his money. As a bonus, you will be able to get more real estate under contract, and closed, as more avenues of finance open for you based on a strong credit rating.

Watch Out for Pitfalls

With the slowing real estate market, some real estate investors are trying to survive financially by refinancing their investment properties, hoping to generate enough cash to keep their heads above water. While that approach may simply serve as a bandage, unless the underlying problem is addressed, the short-term solution could lead to a financially devastating crisis.

There is a widely held real estate investment doctrine that suggests the best way to purchase real estate is maximize the loan amount (over finance it) to get the transaction closed and move on. That is advocated for two reasons. First, it allows for a zero-down approach to investing and second, it can generate cash.

While I believe those two reasons may be valid, they are only insofar as the transaction merits it. The approach works if you are buying significantly below the current market value or if appreciation is rocketing into the stratosphere. In the case of the latter, you should be warned that at some point the rocket always runs out of fuel and crashes back on earth. Take care the rocket doesn't hit you on its downward plummet.

Smart real estate investors resist the temptation to over finance property simply for the sake of generating cash. They have at least three reasons for this.

Reason #1

It's best not to over finance your property because you pay a premium if you exceed 80 percent of the value to the loan amount. Historically, lenders embraced the notion that if their investment (loan) is at that value, or less, the risk is acceptable. If the loan value is more than 80 percent, the loan gets more risky for the lender. That is why PMI (Private Mortgage Insurance) exists. PMI ensures that in the event of a default, the lender will not be liable for a loss in excess of 80 percent.

There is another way to accomplish the same thing. You can get a second mortgage (a note and Deed of Trust) on the property for the amount needed above 80 percent. The interest rate will be higher than the first mortgage, and in some cases much higher, but at least it is tax deductible. There have been some recent proposed changes to the tax deductibility of PMI. Be sure to talk to your mortgage broker before you make a final decision on whether to secure a second mortgage or use PMI.

If you happen to find a 100-percent loan, be forewarned—the payment will eat you alive. The high interest rate charged for a 100-percent loan makes the transaction fundamentally undoable if you are paying retail. If you are considering that option, check and double check the property analysis you will perform to ensure you are making a wise decision.

The bottom line is: the higher percentage of loan amount you borrow, the more you pay for the privilege of borrowing. There is a balancing act here and it will behoove you to learn everything you can about the pros and cons of all of the available financing options.

Reason #2

If you over finance your property, you can't consistently enjoy positive cash flow. For the real estate investor, cash flow is the name of the game. If you compromise by thinking that you will have only an extra $200 to pay out of my pocket each month, you will soon be out of business. If you do that 10 times, you have to come up with $2,000 each month simply to say you're a real estate investor. How smart is that?

Real Estate Investing

I received a call from a friend who has several properties with a negative cash flow. The payments are eating him alive. The call was a request that I take over his payments and he would deed me the house. I couldn't do it because the rent was several hundred dollars less than the payment and I couldn't see a quick exit strategy.

If you don't have positive cash flow (or equity), your options are limited. In addition, your dream of leaving your current job to become a full-time real estate investor is put on hold while you figure a way out of your mess. Those who have gotten themselves into this mess in the first place did so because they either didn't do the math, or didn't do the math correctly.

Reason #3
If your property is over financed, you will have a difficult time getting rid of it if the need arises. My

advice is to make sure you can dump the property easily before you close the purchase transaction.

I also received calls from two separate investors who had property they had to unload. Fortunately for them, they could do it. Their loan to value was about 80 percent with no cash out of pocket when they bought. Both investors sold to me.

As a result of more experience and networking structure, I was able to resell the two houses in less than 48 hours. This was possible in our slowing market because my sellers were into the property without being over financed. I was also able to give my buyers a great deal with great terms that promised positive cash flow.

If your exit strategy does not include a winning situation for your end buyer, you do not have an effective strategy. Use this as a general rule: every transaction has to be a win-win for both parties. If it is not, then you shouldn't buy it.

Financing has its place. I seldom use any of my own money to close a deal. When I do use my money, I know when I'm getting it back. I'm not suggesting that 100-percent financing is wrong for the real estate investor. I'm saying that 100-percent financing is wrong in most cases if you are paying retail.

Any time you find real estate in which to invest at 80 percent of value or less, by all means find a loan for the entire amount if your exit strategy fits the loan. You will have succeeded in creating wealth and probably positive cash flow. Whenever that is possible, take the leap forward. Financing can be a two-edged sword. Over finance and you can find yourself choking to death. Used properly, financing can create wealth to help you realize financial independence, plan for the future, and provide you with the ability to give generously to a worthy cause.

What is Creating Wealth and What is Cash Flow?

Too often beginning real estate investors confuse cash flow with wealth building. It's true that cash flow is essential to filling your wealth bucket; however, you can be building wealth in other ways that do not necessarily rely on cash flow. An example of that would be a long-term rental property. If the rent you collect puts you in a positive cash flow situation (and that could mean only $25 a year), you are still building wealth.

Every rent payment that tenant makes, which you in turn apply to the mortgage on the property, is money that is building your wealth. As long as you keep that property properly maintained, and are careful about who you select as tenants for your long-term rental investments, you should also be experiencing appreciation on that property over time in addition to the equity you are gaining from paying down the mortgage against it.

Long-term rentals are just one possible real estate investment opportunity and the pros and cons of that option are worthy of having a book written specifically on that topic. Many have.

The common denominator between this wealth building scenario and others that I have already provided is that the end result is that you had a working strategy to buy, make money, then if you choose, to get out and take that money to invest in a bigger and better opportunity. "Cash flow" is a generic term that can be used differently depending on the context in which it is used. We are using the term cash flow to mean spendable dollars generated after expenses are paid. Cash flow is most commonly used in real estate investing to evaluate the performance of a particular project or your entire business as a whole.

Creating wealth or wealth building is the dollars that you have earned and can add to your asset portfolio in either dollars or capital. Each time that tenant makes a rent payment on that long-term rental, you have just earned more capital that you can leverage for spendable dollars or sell for spendable dollars. The amount of money in your checking account does not define your total net worth. If you are doing it right, however, you will have significant cash flow and continue building wealth through capital investments simultaneously.

Chapter 15: Types of Real Estate Investing

Purchasing Rental Properties

Like the example just used to define "creating wealth," purchasing rental properties offers many advantages for an investor. Here are a few:

1. The tenant rent payments pay down the mortgage and build your net worth.
2. The equity in that property becomes working capital that you can borrow against and use for financing other investment projects.
3. If you maintain the property, you should realize appreciation during the term of your ownership (assuming that is for a minimum of a few years and you reside in a healthy market).
4. Multiple tax breaks are available for landlords for interest, depreciation, insurance costs, travel costs, repair costs, and utilities.

5. Before you run out and buy your first property, it would be wise for you to do some research in your area regarding tenancy rates, average rents and days on the market for properties similar to the one you are considering, so if you want to exit you have an idea of how long it might take.

A general rule is that if interest rates are down most creditworthy people can afford a mortgage, thus they are homebuyers versus renters. As a result, the vast amount of the renter pool will be those who are not able to secure financing. Nothing is wrong with that. A lot of people find themselves in a financial pinch at least once in their life.

However, you should take appropriate measures regarding tenant rules and regulations so you have the option to evict if their term at your property is causing it to depreciate rather than appreciate. Make sure you reserve the right to stop in at least once a month with a 24-hour notice to perform a property inspection, and exercise that right. You owe it to yourself to protect your investment.

Lease Option

The Rent-to-Own approach (sometimes referred to as Lease Purchase or simply Lease Option) to home ownership is a tool used by landlords use to realize positive cash flow as well as help reduce their tax liability. At the same time, an owner can help families realize their dream of home ownership. The Rent-to-Own approach can be a win-win situation for both parties to the transaction.

Why would a property owner want to sell by Rent-to-Own?

Investment owners enter into a Rent-to-Own for several reasons. For the buyer, a Rent-to-Own option is a form of creative financing that could result in:

1. Low move-in costs. The move-in costs are lower for the potential buyer, usually requiring a security deposit, first months rent, and a small "down payment" (option consideration).
2. Immediate possession of a home. If the home is vacant, you can usually move in as soon as the credit check is complete and initial fees paid.
3. Allows buyer to build a down payment. The option consideration is used for the closing costs and down payment when you purchase. A portion of the rent may go to purchase price, which helps save money.
4. Allows Buyer to repair credit. Time is a great healer of bad credit choices when you seek credit restoration help. If you have filed for bankruptcy or have judgments against you, a lease option allows time to administer first aid to credit.
5. The home usually has a fixed price at the end of the lease. Knowing what the costs will be

when you exercise your option and complete the purchase of the home is important.

6. Permits buyer to move up in neighborhood. You can actually live in an upscale home at a price close to the cost of a less affluent neighborhood. The fact is, the higher the price, the lower the monthly costs in proportion to the value of the home.

7. Appreciation of the home while you are a "tenant." You can actually earn equity in the home you are leasing. If the real estate market is in decline, you can simply walk away without any legal repercussions. In a Rent-to-Own agreement (specifically the option portion), the only obligation is on the part of the landlord to complete the transaction.

Why pay $20,000 or $50,000 down on a property when you can control and use the property with just a few thousand dollars out of pocket that will be applied toward the purchase price when you purchase?

Making the choice of how you want to control property and create wealth can be a difficult decision. It is, however, one that has to be made at some point as you consider whether to rent or own property. In the market of 2007, now is a good time to enter into a Rent-to-Own property. If you are looking for a home and want to own one in the next year or two, why rent when Rent-to-Own has such a tremendous benefit for you?

One of the benefits of renting is that if you don't like your location you can easily move to another one once the lease has ended. There are also drawbacks to renting that lead many people to buy their own home. When you rent, you are paying to live in a space that will never be yours. And then there is the third option we just went over—Rent-to-Own.

Let's touch on all three options now because they are options that you will sometimes need to evaluate in your purchase decisions and they are always options that your buyers will need to evaluate when buying or renting from you.

Each option—buying, renting and lease option—have advantages and disadvantages. When you are deciding about a property purchase as either your residence or an investment, consider the good and bad of either choice. Ultimately, you must decide if the benefits of home buying versus renting or lease option outweigh the associated costs and benefits.

Home Buying

The true cost of home buying is more than the down payment and mortgage. Another consideration is private mortgage insurance (if your down payment was less than 20 percent of the home price), homeowner's insurance, property taxes, and maintenance. Those costs can increase your monthly payment by as much as 40 percent.

On the positive side, in buying the home, each payment you make on your mortgage brings you one-step closer to home ownership. As you pay on your mortgage, you increase the equity in your home. That equity can be beneficial if you want to sell your home or use it to borrow money.

It's a well-known fact that mortgage interest payments and some property taxes are tax deductible. For many, that is a good reason for home buying. Not only are you investing your money in a valuable asset, but also you get a break from the federal government for doing so.

Appreciation is another factor in home buying. That's where you realize profit simply by owning the property and allowing the economy to raise the value of the property. Sometimes that can be significant if you live in an area of rapid price upswing. If you own a property for 10 years, the value of that property will likely double.

When you buy real property, property maintenance becomes your responsibility. You will either have to maintain the home yourself or pay someone to do it. In either case, it is an additional concern and cost that you must take into account.

Renting

In a rental, the landlord provides general maintenance of the property and fixes anything that breaks down. When renting, moving is easier for the tenant. Of course, this depends on the amount of belongings they have, but generally speaking, people who rent tend to have less "stuff" than people who own.

Extra fees are usually nonexistent. Although some landlords require that tenants have renter's insurance, premiums are generally much lower than homeowner's insurance. When you rent, all you have to worry about is the rent and utilities. But you also have to consider that rents go up. That means that tenants will likely be paying more rent year after year.

On the down side, you could rent a home for 30 years and not realize any appreciation or profit. If you had bought rather than rented, in 30 years you would have a sizable asset. I have one tenant who has rented from me for more than 15 years. He has paid for my property. The value of the property has gone from $25,000 to $250,000.

Rent-to-Own or Lease Option

The third way you can control property is through a hybrid alternative. In the Lease Option you control the property for a specified period of time and perhaps even enjoy appreciation without be obligated to actually purchase the home. On a Lease Option, you make a down payment in the form of option consideration that is nonrefundable. The seller will often deduct an agreed-upon amount per month from your purchase price, and you, therefore, built a sort of equity even while renting.

You don't actually have equity, but if you close the purchase you have money built in that helps with the down payment and closing costs. I sometimes refer to this as a "forced savings program" because it forces the buyer/tenant to set aside money in the event he chooses to close the loan.

Remember to do the math and to take the numbers at face value. You don't want to gamble on investments that don't look good on paper, even if you think all it really needs is your magic touch. Too many options are available that are a sure solid investment. Move on to those.

Lease Option as an Investment Strategy
Speaking directly to the investment side of purchasing, I think the lease-option strategy may be a perfect real estate investment vehicle for new investors. No other approach offers the kind of return on investment when a person is just starting out and has limited funds and investment knowledge.

Through a lease-option strategy, a person with little or no money can control a property and enjoy appreciation while experiencing an up-front cash flow as well as a positive monthly cash flow. I've written and spoken about these three aspects on several occasions. Not only can you make money, you can do so without the headache of being a landlord if you have the right documents. I have several lease-options in force at this writing and never get a call from a buyer tenant. When I was a traditional landlord, I regularly received calls from tenants.

A lease-option is an investment strategy that consists of two parts. One part is a lease, the agreement to possess "equitable title," which essentially means you have the right to live in and use the property free from interference as long as you pay as agreed. The other part is an option to purchase the property. In an option, the tenant buyer has the right, but not an obligation, to purchase the property at a later date.

When I'm a lease-option seller, I always try to get at least $5,000 down in nonrefundable money called option consideration. That sum is applied to the purchase price if the tenant-buyer exercises his option and purchases the house after the lease expires. I also try to get at least $200 each month in monthly positive cash flow. That cash flow is spendable dollars after expenses.

I spent $1,200 to have my attorney draw up lease and option agreements that has essentially ended all middle-of-the-night repair calls. If you purchased on a lease-option with the right to sublet (also called a sandwich lease), you can have the same benefit.

It seems that life is perfect when you have the right agreements in place, but be careful. While all of this might sound great, there is a downside. Things can go wrong, causing you to lose both sleep and money. You could lose the house you leased or optioned and you could get sued for not living up to your agreement with the tenant-buyer.

How do you protect yourself from these possibilities?

1. Check the Title. If you are buying by way of a lease option, be sure you do your due diligence. Have a preliminary title report done (in my hometown, it's called a lot book report if you just want to check the title). You may find that your seller doesn't own the property or that he has so many liens against the property that you will never be able to buy it. The money you spend here is money well spent. You can also do the research yourself if you have the time to go to the county recorder and go though documents.
2. Check Credit. If you are the seller, be sure to run a credit check on your tenant-buyer. If you are the buyer, run a credit check on the seller. You will be surprised what you will find. Rule of thumb: Know as much about the buyer or the seller as you can before you sign

documents. It is said that knowledge is power. My advice: Be knowledgeable.

3. Escrow. If I'm a lease-option buyer, I want to open an escrow account. I will open it with several documents. I will include a completely filled out purchase agreement (as an exhibit) describing the terms of the purchase along with a one-page lease-option agreement. I have the seller sign a warranty deed to place in escrow.

4. If he is off sailing in the China Sea when I get ready to close the transaction, I won't have to find him. Also, sellers sometimes experience seller's remorse before your lease it up. A signed warranty deed will avoid this problem. In the event of a legal action or challenge, that paper work creates a paper trail that spells out the intent of the buyer and the seller when the transaction took place.

5. Option Money. I always get enough nonrefundable option consideration to cover costs if my tenant-buyer wants to cheat me out

of money. So far, I've never lost any money nor had a house damaged by a buyer tenant.

6. The more money your tenant-buyer puts down, the safer you probably are. The approach I use to get plenty of money down is to constantly refer to the tenant-buyer as a buyer. I let him know that I'm not looking for a tenant, I want a buyer. That usually separates those who want to rent from those who want to buy. The buyer mentality is much better for you than that of a tenant. Rule of thumb: If you are buying on a lease-option, use as little of your own money as possible. If you are selling, ask for as much as you think you can get to protect yourself and create cash flow. I always start by asking for $5,000 cash, or cash and part trade.

7. Lease-Option Agreement. Use good, solid documents for your lease-option agreements. If I'm a lease option buyer I use a one-page Lease Option form. There are legal reasons for

that: I do not want a document too specific if I am the buyer. If I am a lease-option seller, I use very detailed lease agreements and a separate detailed option agreement and I caution my protégés to not use generic forms from an office supply store or free downloadable forms off the Internet when they are the seller. Remember, the stronger and tighter the documents when you sell, the better. When you are the buyer, use a one-page document.

8. Notice of Option. If you are the buyer in a lease option transaction, record a Notice of Option (it may also be call a Memorandum of Option) with your county clerk. For a few dollars in recording fees, you can go on record that you have an interest in the property. If the seller tries to sell the house from under you, you can stop the proceeding with that document. If your Option Agreement and Notice of Option have the right wording, you

can even stop your seller from borrowing more money on the property.

9. Insurance. If you are a lease-option buyer, have a letter prepared for the seller to sign that you can mail to his insurance agent that instructs him to include you as an additional insured "as your interest may appear." This may save you money in the event of a loss due to fire or liability claim. If you are the seller, advise your tenant-buyer in writing to obtain rental insurance to protect their personal property in the event of a loss. The steps outlined are not all-inclusive, but they will get you started down the path of self-protection. People who lose money in lease options are those who have failed to protect themselves by using the properly worded documents.

Hybrid Consumer

The lease-option market is huge. We market to a hybrid customer—not a buyer and not a tenant. We look for someone who wants to buy a house but forced to rent for one reason or another. We are looking for the person who has a credit problem, for example, and who believes he can't qualify for a home loan.

An ever-increasing number of people have credit problems. I run ads that invite people to the web site, and the response is good. When close to completing new projects, my financial lending partner and I will hold Saturday seminars for people who want more information about buying through a lease-option. By the end of the meeting, we generally have a long list of qualified people who sign up to become a tenant-buyer.

Risk versus Return on Investment
If you think you'll have sleepless nights worrying about whether a house will be leased when it gets done, you should not buy an investment house. If you don't understand what is going on, you should not buy an investment of any kind.

Again, real estate investing involves risk. However, after you look at the facts, the risks are minimal, and I believe they are less risky than anything else available when you consider the return on your cash investment.

If you invest $5,000, for example, and achieve a return of $30,000, what is your rate of return? You would earn a 100-percent return on your money if you realized a $10,000 profit. If you made $20,000, you would realize a 200-percent return. If you made $30,000, your return on investment would be 300 percent. I would put my money in the bank if I could earn 300 percent instead of the 2 percent I earn in a savings account today.

If you had a strategy to get your $5,000 returned, and you succeeded and made $30,000, your return on your investment would be infinite. For zero cash, you make $30,000. That is a good deal in anyone's book.

Icing on the Cake

I once offered an option for people who are new to real estate investing and feel they need a safety net and mentor. For those who have partnered with me (they serve as a financial partner by putting down a $5,000 deposit and securing the financing), I offered a guarantee. I personally returned the $5,000 deposit within 30 days of closing of the long-term loan.

What that meant was that my partner had no cash in the project. I still take on partners, but I no longer use this strategy as outlined here. Now I simply offer to partner with them with no personal guarantee. I have discovered that it is much better when your partner has money in a project.

Assignment of Contracts and Bank Short Sales

You found a good real estate buy and have a motivated seller who wants out of his house yesterday. Mr. Seller agreed to your purchase offer of $275,000 for his home appraised at $350,000. That is a good deal for Mr. Seller because he purchased another home and the bank will take the house back if he can't unload it soon.

Your plan is to flip the house. You are going to pick up a few dollars in the transaction and sell it to someone looking for a property to purchase wholesale. But how do you get paid for finding a buyer without seasoning the purchase (owning it for a specified period of time)?

Lenders and some title companies are really jumpy right now about such a transaction. A member of the investment club I lead introduced me to strategy called a Reverse Assignment.

Here is how it works:

1. Step One: You find a good deal and Mr. Seller agrees to the price and terms of your offer.
2. Step Two: You disclose to Mr. Seller that you are an investor and your plan is to find a buyer

who will take over the contract and close the sale in escrow.

3. Step Three: "But," Mr. Seller objects, "How can you accomplish this task when I have been unable to do so?" "Because I'm a professional. This is what I do!" you explain. Mr. Seller gets the point and says, "Okay, let's do it." You add your fee (whatever that might be—$1,000, $5,000, etc.—don't get too greedy or you won't find a buyer) to the purchase price and Mr. Seller signs a promissory note that is payable at closing for that amount. Now your contract price is $280,000 ($275,000 plus your fee of $5,000).

4. Step Four: You find a buyer (Ms. Buyer). Ms. Buyer agrees to purchase the home for $280,000 by way of your Assignment of Contract and applies for a loan with her lender.

5. Step Five: Ms. Buyer and Mr. Seller go to the title company to sign the closing documents. Since you have presented to the title company

the promissory note Mr. Seller signed, you will be paid through escrow when the new loan is funded. Is Ms. Buyer happy? Yes. She purchased a home worth $350,000 for $280,000 and in essence created $70,000 in equity. Is Mr. Seller happy? Yes. He has unloaded a tremendous weight off his shoulders and has rid himself of the alligator that was eating him alive. Are you happy? Definitely, because you get paid!

Notice that seven things were accomplished:

1. Mr. Seller got his price.
2. Ms. Buyer got a great deal.
3. The deal did not require seasoning.
4. The appraisal amount requested was the original contract amount.
5. There is no feeling from Ms. Buyer that you were ripping her off because you didn't have to ask her to write a check in the amount of $5,000 for the assignment, which could have resulted in her going directly to Mr. Seller to cut a deal.

6. You got paid.
7. You are free to look for another great deal so that you can create more positive cash flow that will enable you to give more to your favorite charity/cause, pay your monthly bills, or build up your retirement account—or all of the above.

Tax Liens and Tax Deed Purchases

Tax deeds are sold in 35 states throughout the United States. Almost every state has a method in place for recouping back taxes from delinquent taxpayers. Bidding and buying tax liens and tax deeds at government sales can be quite profitable.

Every homeowner must pay some sort of real estate tax to the government. If a homeowner fails to pay the required taxes on the property, the county will offer the property up for sale at an auction to help generate the lost tax income. During a tax deed sale, the property is usually sold for the back tax amount plus any fees, interest charges, and court costs. Because property taxes are a small percentage of market value, investors purchasing a tax deed can acquire full property rights at a fraction of the market price.

By law, tax deed sales must be announced to the public and are usually sold to the highest bidder. The winning bidder purchases the deed to property and becomes the new owner—obtaining all rights to the property, clear of encumbrances such as any mortgages, liens, or deeds of trust.

The tax lien and tax deed processes may be distinguished by what is referred to as the bundle of rights sold to the purchaser. In states using a tax deed system, county governments will sell full ownership rights to the investor. As of 2007, 17 states authorize the sale of ownership rights to tax delinquent property through a tax deed sale.

Conversely, in so-called tax lien states, county governments sell only their right to the tax lien or tax claim on the real property. A total of 18 states have authorized sales of a county tax lien position to the public. A property tax lien is secured to real property as a first priority claim. The end result is a highly secured investment that is typically appreciating and can also be sold for more than you paid.

As with any real estate investment, you should thoroughly research the property involved in the tax deed or lien sale before making any offer. Do your homework and bid smart. You should also view the property and research its value before you bid. Another important point is that you should clearly understand what ownership rights you are purchasing through this sale. Each state has slightly different procedures, and remembering that not every state offers the same type of sale is important.

To find the dates and times for these types of sales, contact the county office where you want to purchase a tax deed or lien and check the local area newspaper. Words of advice, however. Stay local until you completely understand the process and what you stand to gain and lose.

Building a New Home for Lease or Sale

If I am considering building a house as an investment, I want to begin by first asking if it is possible to create wealth by building a house. The second thing I want to know, and it's almost as important, is can I create wealth without using my cash reserves? If I conclude that, yes, it is possible, then I want to find out how it works. So, let's take a look.

The figures below are used for illustration purposes only. You may insert your local information in the place of my numbers. The equation will work for your geographical area.

Let's assume that you find a building lot for the sum of $100,000, and you have a builder under contract to build you a house for $124,000. It would look like this:

Real Estate Investing

Building Lot: $100,000

Cost of House (total): $124,000

Total Cost: $224,000

You want the house and land to appraise at about $300,000. Do you know why? You want the construction loan to be about 80 percent or less of the appraised cost. That assumes you have a lender who will loan you 80 percent of appraised value—not 80 percent of cost. If your lender will not loan on the appraised value, find one who will.

There are at least two good reasons you want the 80-percent loan to appraised value. First, it's easier to get a construction loan and "take out" loan if the value is an 80/20 split. The lender will look at the 20-percent equity position and rightly believe their risk is less than a 100-percent loan to appraised value loan. In other words, if you have a 20-percent position, you are less likely to walk away and leave the lender to pick up the pieces.

Second, the day you sign the contract with the builder, you know that you have created wealth. In the example above, you created $60,000. If you build two of these houses in one year, you created $120,000. In essence, once you have a builder, floor plan, and lender, and you arranged the appraisal that makes the project work, you created $120,000 with a couple of phone calls.

It's also possible to add your closing costs to the construction loan, and enough money to pay the interest for 6 months during construction. That means little or no money out of your pocket while adding $74,000, or more, per project.

One valid question is: Don, have you ever done this? The answer is, yes. At this writing, I have under contract more than 137 houses where this principle is in play. The exciting thing is that you can do it, also.

The Appraisal

What happens if the appraisal comes back with a figure that is at the cost of building? This does happen occasionally and when it does, I pass on the project. However, if you perform your due diligence, you should know before you spend the money on an appraisal how the figures will work.

Do an "Arms Length" Appraisal

I call my mortgage broker and ask her to call the appraiser and ask for information. I do this to have an arm's length transaction so that no one can claim collusion between the appraiser and me. It also simplifies things for the appraisers to deal with just one person.

After you run the numbers you have to determine if the amount of wealth you can create is sufficient for you to go ahead. For me, personally, anything less than $35,000 to is too risky. I have seen eager novices willing to jump at the chance of a $10,000 profit margin, not considering that if just one thing goes wrong, which is always a possibility, the additional costs exceed that amount.

As you can see, when using the new construction model wealth can be created without putting up a lot of your own money.

Rehabilitate a Resale Home and Sell for Profit

Flipping, the real estate investment vehicle in which you purchase a property below value and soon sell it for a profit is a very good way to generate positive cash flow. Flipping has become a big business. I encourage my protégées to buy and sell for a profit without getting into the rehabilitation business if their goal is to be an investor. In some states, you cannot fix and flip unless you are a licensed contractor. In those states, you must generally attend courses, pass a test, and become a member in the state contractors association. The rules and regulations surrounding this topic vary from state to state. Many states, however, still do not require that you are a contractor to do the work yourself.

The biggest mistake that most "fix and flippers" make is that they estimate how much it would cost someone else to make the improvements that you could do for less and then add that amount to their purchase price and voila, that's the correct price for the house. Major mistake. Knowing how to correctly calculate margins and profits on a fix and flip property is the difference between success and failure.

Holding costs are probably the biggest culprit for eating away profit. Too often some very expensive costs associated with fix-and-flip projects are overlooked until it's too late. For example, if it takes 60 to 90 days to do the fixit portion of a flip, then you incur 2 to 3 months in finance charges and holding costs. If it takes another 60 to 90 days to sell your project house once you complete the project, it you are now negative 5 to 6 months of holding costs.

Holding costs are loan payment, interest payment, taxes and insurance (and PMI insurance if that was needed). Before you make a fix-and-flip decision, call your lender and find out what it will cost you each month to carry the house while you're rehabilitating it. That calculation should include worst-case scenario rehabilitation time and days on the market. Deduct that total right off the top.

Wait, we're not done yet! Are you going to sell your completed project as a For Sale by Owner or are you going to list it with an agent? If you are going to list it with an agent, you should assume the average national commission rate of 6 percent. Now, add the rest of the closing costs such as title insurance and transfer fees.

If you're going to attempt to sell your fix and flip as a For Sale by Owner then you need to put together your own marketing and advertising plan. Where are you going to print ads? How much are those ads going to cost? You can also typically assume that if you are not listing your property on the Multiple Listing Service (MLS) where it can be accessed by all

Realtors®, then your days on the market are likely going to be a lot more than the listed average. Plan for that because it will add to your holding costs.

In a fix-and-flip project, you also need to plan for at least an extra 10 percent in rehabilitation costs than your original estimate included. You never know what you are going to uncover in a fix-and-flip property, so you need to plan for that.

Now, if you have appropriately considered finance and holding charges, closing costs, unexpected issues, and commissions or marketing costs, you are much closer to determining what you really need to sell your rehabilitated home to break even. That's right, what are you working for if you don't plan profit for yourself? As a general rule, assume that you need to net at least 10 percent of the total sell price of the home in order for it to make sense. So add that to the costs column and NOW you have your sell price.

Stop! Before you say "Ok, I'll just sell it for that much then." The market doesn't work that way. You should determine how much homes with similar square footage and of the same age and proximity have sold for in the last 6 months. A house is worth only what someone is willing to pay. The buyer determines the price—not the seller. If buyers aren't paying what you want, your efforts will be fruitless and costly.

Once you have done the research and determined the correct selling price range, attempt to price your fix and flip on the lower end of that range so you can keep the days on the market as low as possible. Remember, each month you sit on the property is another month of financing charges that were taken right of your profits. Holding out for best price is a fallacy that will come back to bite you every time.

Another obvious consideration for fix-and-flip projects is the skill and resources required to do the job. Some people really can do it all and know how to do electrical, plumbing, lay tile, and knock down walls or re-drywall.

Most however, do not. If you are one of those people you need to take a serious look at what you will be putting into the project in time and labor. If you are not, you must get accurate estimates from professionals to ensure the work is done correctly. It all comes back to being honest with yourself about what the project will cost. If it doesn't make sense on paper, don't massage the numbers until it does. If it doesn't make sense, move on and find a project that does.

One other thing to consider for a fix-and-flip project is that it takes a lot of your time. Even if you hire the skilled labor, you are still the general contractor and have a great amount of responsibility. Remember that there are only so many hours in a day. Ask yourself if there is something else you could be doing (flip for profit versus fix and flip) that will make you more money in a shorter amount of time.

I am not trying to discourage you from using the fix-and-flip approach to real estate investing. I merely want to make sure you are aware of the pitfalls for novices. Don't fall into these traps. If you do want to pursue such an option, by all means, do it. But do yourself a favor and start small and start smart.

Perhaps your first project should be one that requires little more than aesthetic changes. A lot of dated homes need a fresh coat of paint inside and out and new flooring throughout.

Replace light fixtures as well as kitchen and bath countertops and you have yourself a fresh feeling home, ready to move into, and worth a great deal more in the buyer's eyes than it was when you bought it.

You can keep your costs down, do most of the work yourself, and still learn the basics of how the fix-and-flip process works. Perhaps you'll only make a couple of thousand dollars on the first one, but at least you will have learned the basics without going backwards!

Fix and flip can be a very viable method of real estate investing. The trick to doing it correctly is doing the numbers correctly. You have to be extra cautious with your purchase decisions to ensure you have a solid home that will be worth the list price you will need to ask to make your desired profit. Do the research regarding average days on the market, fair market value, improvement estimates, holding costs, and sales and marketing costs before you make a purchase decision. Time is money. Each day you have possession of that property is another day of holding costs you incur and comes off your bottom line.

Buy smart, be honest with yourself about the numbers, and fix and flip as quickly as possible to achieve the highest possible profit. Start small so you can learn the ropes and build yourself a rotary card file of resources and skilled contacts. Make sure that every improvement is geared toward the largest possible audience (neutral colors, nothing too far out of the ordinary). For an extra special touch, stage the home (bring in furnishing) when you are finished. That will be your chance to show off your natural ability to decorate while putting money in your pocket.

Building Your Resource Team

I included a chart that illustrates what your team should look like. Don't fill these positions with just anyone. It is imperative that you accept nothing less than the best! You need team members who understand your long-term objectives, have resources of their own, and want to create a long-term relationship.

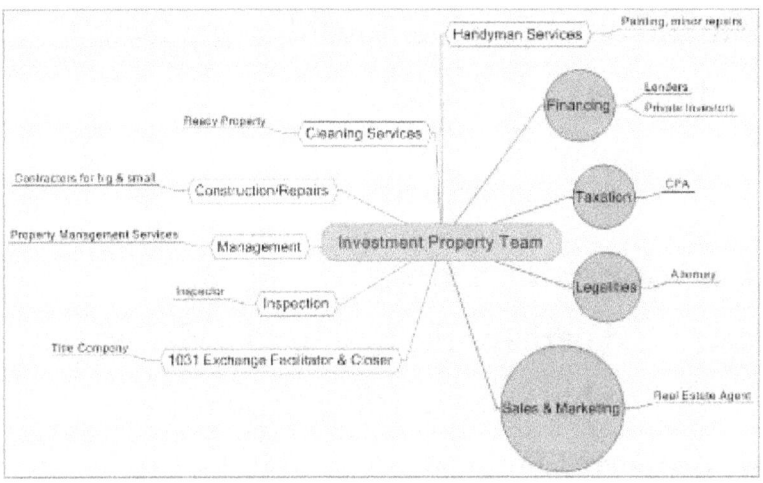

Chapter 16: Finding a "Good Deal"

I'm often asked, how do you find good deals? I had a new protégé demand, "Why should I go out and look at the property? You're supposed to find me a good deal." She failed to understand that if I found a "good deal," I would buy it!

First, let's define what constitutes a "good deal." To you, that may seem obvious, but if you can't clearly define what it means to you, how do you know when you've found one? Consider the following factors when defining what a good deal means to you.

What is your exit strategy?
One factor and perhaps the first to consider is your exit strategy. What are you going to do with a specific property? Is the strategy to hold, flip, lease option, wholesale, fix and flip, or?

Before I close a transaction, I know what I'm going to do with the property. Sometimes my strategy changes, but for the most part it pretty much remains the same. If I find a duplex in my home town that I can pick up for 60 percent of value I will clean it up, hold it long term (more than 12 months), and then sell it.

If the duplex happens to be in Klamath Falls, Oregon, which is about a 3-hour drive south from where I live, I will likely sell it with great owner terms for a small profit and move it quickly. I will take that approach because I don't want to manage property that far away.

What are your goals?

Each of us has goals unique to us. I teach my protégés to write a life purpose statement and build goals around that. Once you understand your purpose, you are in a much better position to define your goals and develop a plan to achieve those goals.

If your goal is to create passive positive cash flow of $10,000 each month so you can live on $5,000 and give away $5,000 to philanthropic projects, then you need to manage your activity and focus on your objectives in a way that will enhance your ability to achieve the over all goal.

Let's suppose then, that an opportunity comes along that would take you in a different direction.

Although it's a great opportunity, it might not be in your best interest if not aligned with your life purpose.

What are your skills?

If you don't know the difference between a power drill and a chain saw, you had better stay away from houses and apartment units that need to be repaired before you rent them. Unless you are looking at a property with an eye toward learning something new, stay clear of properties that require skills you are unable or unwilling to provide. The investment opportunity may not be as good at it appears.

What is your financial strength?

This one is a biggie. I've seen new real estate investors get deep into debt and unable to complete transactions because they tried to purchase a good deal, only to lose it and other property as well.

For example, unless you have deep pockets, you may want to stay away from vacant land. Investing in vacant land and building lots is a rich person's market—unless you are building houses as a strategy. There is generally no inward cash flow to help offset the flow of cash out. The good deal suddenly goes sour when you run out of money and lose all you invested in the good deal.

If you have limited resources, try to keep your investment purchases to single family homes at the lower end of the real estate investment spectrum—or a step above. Many more retail buyers and tenants are at this level, which means you have a greater chance of selling the house or filling a vacancy and ultimately realize a positive stream of income.

I know several people who got in trouble when they found a "great deal." They borrowed to the hilt and made payments on empty houses. That strategy will set you up for financial disaster. It matters little that you picked up a $900,000 house for $700,000 if you cannot find a buyer or make the payments for an extended period of time. The deal may be good for someone, but is it a good deal for you?

As you can see, the term good deal is relative. Lots of good deals may be out there, but be sure the deal is good for you. This segment is a reiteration, in a different way, of the segment that tells you that you have to run the numbers.

I've said it before and I'll say it again. If it doesn't make sense on paper, then it doesn't make sense. You are, after all, investing. Risk is involved; however, you can minimize that risk dramatically by asking the right questions, doing an analysis, and acting accordingly.

If you are eager for customers to be contacting you instead of your having to find every one of them, you may want to give this some serious thought early on, not later. Remember, however, marketing costs money. I have seen new business owners go under because their marketing budget wasn't properly in line with their sales. Plan big, budget small, and be creative.

Marketing Plan Research: An overview of your market.

- What is the total size of your market or markets?
- What companies within your industry have succeeded and how?

Customers: Who are your customers?

- What are their values, attitudes, and beliefs?
- Are they local, regional, national, or international?

- Are they liberal or conservative?
- Are they rich or financially challenged?
- Can you envision your client?
- Will you target other consumers, other businesses or the government?

Competition: Who is your competition?

- Do your competitors have Web sites? If yes, list the domain names. Make a list of what you like and don't like about their sites.
- What are your competitor's strengths?
- What are your competitor's weaknesses?

Your Company Strengths: What gives you the confidence that you will succeed?

- What unique benefits does your product, service, or cause provide?
- How have you branded your company so you will be remembered? Think positioning

slogans such as, "Let your fingers do the walking" or "Finger lickin' good." Are market indicators in your favor?
- Do you have a top-notch management team?
- Are market demographics definitely in your favor?

Your Company Weaknesses

- Are you underfinanced?
- Do you lack technological know-how?
- Can you find all the right people for the jobs if you are outrageously successful?
- Do you have an adequate facility?
- Do you have ready access to your goods supplies or suppliers?
- Do you foresee any intellectual property problems?

Online Web site Promotion

How do you plan to promote your site? Give a detailed listing of each effort along with its timeline.

Are you going to use "pay per click" Search Engines?

Are you going to hire a Search Engine Marketing company?

Do you have an online public relations plan?

Are you going to conduct an on going linking effort?

Do you plan to have weekly, bi-weekly, or monthly specials?

Are you going to do anything promotional?

Are you planning ongoing email campaigns?

Off-line Promotions

Newspaper, magazine, radio, or television advertising campaign?

Public relations campaign?

Catalog, brochure, or direct mailings?

Budget
- Have you set a budget for your marketing?
- If yes, how far out did you plan the expenditures?
- How much will you outsource? If so, who will you use?
- How do you plan to generate the money to fuel your ongoing efforts?

Chapter 17: Doing a Buy/Sell Analysis

Easy Math

Doing a buy/sell analysis for an investment property can be done many ways. If you spend some time researching the topic on the Internet, you will find hundreds and perhaps thousands of sites that offer software programs or kits for helping solve all of your problems and make the analysis as easy as pushing a button.

First of all, do you really want the analysis to run itself with little input from you? As I have explained in different parts of this book, you are your own boss and you are responsible for your own success. It is important that you understand why you would decide to either purchase or not purchase a property.

You need to be able to see the bottom line as well as understand why the bottom line says what it says. The variables for making purchase decisions for various types of real estate investing tend to fluctuate. You must understand which variables are more important to what types of investing. Also important is that you understand the financial aspect of this business so you can gain financing.

Your lender, if you go that route, will have a specific set of criteria required for funding. If the criteria are not met, he must go through his board or chain of command for approval. They will be even less responsive to a poor or high-risk financial analysis than the loan officer.

If, however, one criterion for assessing risk is a little off, and you know why it is off, you can explain how your exit strategy for that property will make the factor a non-issue. If you can't explain the details of the financial side of the business, you will not be nearly as successful in the lending layer.

Let me tell you a secret. Lots of people hate math. The truth is you do not have to be an accountant to understand the basics of real estate investment analysis or lending criteria. But I won't lie to you either. You will save yourself many headaches in the long run if you take the time to learn some formulas frequently used in the real estate industry. Think of it as taking a nighttime cold medicine when you have a cold. It's horrible going down, but once you've made yourself do it, you are so thankful that you did because you will be able to rest so much easier.

As I mentioned, you will come across multiple analysis methods for real estate investment in your future research in this industry. I'll briefly describe for you the importance of specific areas in the spreadsheet.

The very first section captures the cost of the property, the down payment you must apply toward that amount, the interest rate, the term of the loan, and the purchase date. With this information included, you can calculate your principal and interest payment (commonly known as P&I). Obviously, the P&I payments are just one element of your monthly expenses but should be considered first and forefront.

The next two sections of the spreadsheet are about calculating depreciation deductions you can take because you own this rental property. Depreciation is one of the perks of being a real estate investor—ultimately putting more cash in your pocket. Using Uncle Sam's math, the deductions are valid and legal, which you can subtract directly from your gross income on the property, balancing the playing field a little.

Your income from the investment is coming from the rent you receive (in this long-term holding strategy analysis). It is always a good idea to investigate and find out vacancy rates in your local area and include an impact. If you plan for that up front, then you will help you be financially prepared.

The annual operating expenses portion of this spreadsheet is straightforward, and the purpose of this section is to remind you that you need to consider each category in relationship to your annual expense before proceeding. If you're simply "running some figures in your head," you might forget something that will come out of your pocket later. Use the spreadsheet and do the analysis.

If you fill in the information up to that point correctly, you can set up a spreadsheet like Figure 3 to populate the balance of the information. But, before you do that, be sure you understand what exactly you are populating when you will in the fields.

Your Gross Operating Income is your total income before expenses. It's usually a healthy number, and you will often hear investors who are "talking big" around one another throw those numbers around. Understand right now that those numbers mean nothing about the success of your business.

Operating Expenses in the analysis section of the spreadsheet is a reflection of the sum total of those specifics I encouraged you to review and accurately itemize. Those costs are the costs of holding the property with the exception of your principal and interest payment.

That calculation will lead you to your Net Operating Income. What you see here, if you're following along with the spreadsheet, is that although the terms sound fancy, they are really very simple math. It's more a matter of memorizing what formula each one means than being able to run algebra in your head.

The next step captures the reduction of your loan payment, which encompasses P&I payments. Once you deduct that additional expense, you have what is called

Cash Flow Before Tax. This number is a very important number. If it is negative you need to turn and walk away now. If it is positive even a little, you're making an investment that will earn you money.

The next step in this spreadsheet points out that P&I is not all money in your pocket. The only money in your pocket from P&I payments (your monthly mortgage payment) is the principal reduction part, much like the mortgage on your own home. Bear in mind that the real investment in rental property is the principal reduction you are gaining by using tenant rents to pay that mortgage. They are buying the property for you. If you keep that property in fair and working condition and do necessary improvements, that benefit of your investment will continue to be the strongest return on your invested dollar.

If you bring the Net Operating Expense that you calculated in part one of the analysis section, subtract interest (which is deductible), and subtract depreciation (which is also deductible), you then have your taxable income. Multiply that by your tax bracket and the total will be the amount of money that you have to pay Uncle Sam or that you saved yourself by properly using the deductions that are available to you as a landlord.

You will also see that appreciation can be considered and calculated into this analysis to give you a return on your investment (ROI) percentage with appreciation. My advice is that in a long-term rental analysis, always assume the worst— it will never appreciate. If you do take care of it, it likely will appreciate, which can have a dramatic impact on the return on your investment. But, be level headed and assume a worse case scenario for your risk protection. If it never appreciates, and the return on your investment without appreciation is say….more than 10 percent, is that a good return on investment?

That question is for you to answer. If you have money in a 401K and you are averaging a 7-to-8 percent return then yes, it's not too bad. If you have money in a savings account earning 2 percent, it's great. If you have another investment opportunity where you can earn a greater return in shorter time with those same dollars, then no, it's not a good investment.

Even the very best analysis, whether the basic spreadsheet like this, or some complicated software sold through a convention speaker who charges thousands of dollars to come through the door, the bottom line is the same. You need to understand the formulas and the reason each of those formulas reaches the number that it does. You don't need to know how to actually calculate a specific set of numbers in your head; you simply need to know what the formulas mean, and more importantly, what those numbers mean to you specifically.

In my opinion, the most important formulas for you to concentrate on are the ones that bring you to your return on investment percentages. They are an easy way of measuring your time and energy versus profit.

If your individual retirement account (IRA) is earning you 12 percent all day, every day, and you don't have to lift a finger, then you need to find "deals" that earn you more than that—or you are better off investing more money in your IRA than in your investment business.

That seems like a very simple analogy, and it is. The truth is that if you did 12 deals in 1 week with a 10-percent return, then you are still doing something right. But in the beginning, think of the process at a basic level, and it will minimize your risks and improve your chances for long-term success.

As strongly as I feel about return on investment, lenders often refer to multiple other formulas on a regular basis, many of which take priority, in their opinion over return on investment. For that reason, and to broaden your insight to the various methods of measuring the risk of an investment, learning some of the formulas is important. Use them on fictitious examples until you understand how one can impact another and what variable in the total equation that impacts the outcome of that formula.

According to Frank Gallinelli, the author of What Every Real Estate Investor Needs to Know About Cash Flow . . . and 36 Other Key Financial Measures, there are 37 financial measurements to consider. I believe this is a great book and one you should add to your library as a reference guide, but I am not advocating that you memorize the 37 formulas. I will focus on the most important (most common).

The Closest Thing to a Crystal Ball

So far I have covered a few very important financial measurements in the spreadsheet and will touch on them again to help bring the picture together.

Gross Income is total dollars earned. In this example it is the rent that you collect.

Real Estate Investing

Net Operating Income is the total dollars earned after expenses with the exception of financing and taxes.

Cash Flow is total earnings after subtracting all expenses plus finance charges (mortgage P&I payment). It is the total dollars in minus the total dollars out before the calculation of income tax.

Taxable Income is the income on which you must pay taxes. It is cash flow minus your deductions, such as depreciation and interest.

Capitalization Rate (Cap Rate) is the rate at which you discount future income to determine its present value. Knowing what the cap rates are for your particular type of property in your geographic area is important. Your commercial lender can provide you with that number. The Web site, www.realtyrates.com, can also provide that information.

The formula for cap rate is Net Operating Income divided by Purchase Cost. You can use this formula in three ways using those three variables. If you know the Net Operating Cost and have a target cap rate then you can calculate Purchase Cost. If you have the cap rate and purchase cost but do not know the Net Operating Income, you can calculate that. Banks and lenders throw the cap rate term around regularly. So take the time to really understand this formula.

Cash on Cash is another bank and lender favorite. The easiest explanation for cash on cash is the rate of return you receive on the dollars invested (your down payment) in any one given year. The calculation is cash flow before tax divided by cash invested, and it is a percentage. That formula is a measurement for evaluating how much you are making on the dollars you had to contribute to evaluate if they are in the best place. Could they be making more somewhere else?

Gross Multiplier is a measurement that does not take all variables into consideration. The figure ignores the time value of money and ignores the total operating costs, so it should never be used as a single indicator for purchase.

The Gross Multiplier is the List Price (asking price) divided by the gross operating income (the total of all rent collected annually). Because list price is very market driven, so is the Gross Multiplier. If the Gross Multiplier is too high then the price is too high. For basic consideration, 4 is too low and 10 is too high. Do a couple of these on properties you know are good investments to establish a basic range for your geographic area. Because this is an easy math equation, you may find yourself doing this one "on the spot," which is fine, but remember it does not capture everything.

You can use it to quickly determine if you will not be proceeding without further analysis. If the Gross Multiplier is out of whack, your final analysis will only prove it to be worse, not better.

Return on Investment (ROI) or Return on Equity (ROE) is your income after taxes divided by cash invested (your down payment). It is a method of evaluating if you are earning a great enough return on your dollars invested in this project. If you could be earning more somewhere else, you need to consider getting out.

The measurements I just discussed are the most important financial measurements. Not only because they are the most widely referred to but also because if used together, they provide a comprehensive evaluation of whether or not to proceed with this investment property.

Of course, no calculator, spreadsheet, or software program can capture the variables that only you are capable of capturing, such as condition, location, and current market conditions. If all of those numbers come out perfectly but a new highway is planned to go through the back yard, the numbers are meaningless.

If you master these measurements before you make your first purchase, you will be more educated than a lot of "real estate investors". Don't be one of those investors. Set yourself apart from the crowd before you even start.

Recognize that if you want to do this right and if you want to be successful, you are going to need to commit to educate yourself, to some degree, in all of the layers of real estate investing. Again, no one is suggesting that you learn how the microwave actually works, but if you don't know how to use all of the features then you are likely wasting a lot of time.

If You Want the Cash

You do not have to reinvest 100 percent of the net sales proceeds from the sale of one of your investment properties. The amount you do not reinvest will, however, be subject to depreciation recapture and capital gain income tax liabilities. For tax purposes, the amount you reinvest can be deferred. Pulling some of the proceeds from the next investment purchase is referred to as trading down in value.

When selling your relinquished property, you can carry an installment note. In what is commonly referred to as a carry back note, the note can either be included as part of your 1031 Exchange transaction or executed by you outside of the transaction. The transaction is a complex procedure and should always be reviewed with your legal and tax counsel before moving forward.

If you are looking for cash to put toward your next investment project or anything at all, you can complete the Forward 1031 Exchange process in a normal way, and when you buy your next property, buy it right. In other words, buy a property appraised for much higher than the sale price and refinance that property, pulling cash from the property in the refinance process. If you have good-paying tenants and you don't borrow so much that you are in a negative cash flow situation with that property, you have just secured cash not subject to capital gains taxes. Again, make sure you talk to your lender, accountant, and attorney before proceeding.

There are many other aspects to a 1031 Exchange to consider, such as business entity types in relationship the process, or trusts, and other forms of holdings and how an Exchange impacts them. However, I believe this is a very good place to wrap it up. If you take only one thing away from this chapter, let it be that if you are smart, and if you really want to become wealthy in real estate investing, you need to learn when and how to use a 1031 Exchange or employ someone who will do it for you. The 1031 Exchange is a completely legal way of deferring capital gains taxes, thus keeping more spendable dollars in your pocket. Many great books specific to 1031 Exchanges are available, and I recommend you buy one or two for your resource library.

Chapter 18: Review Your Business Plan

A business plan is only as good as the person who executes it. If you write a business plan that projects a specific amount of income over a specific amount of time, your business plan also needs to drill down to a level that can be executed. For example, if you require 12 sales a year to meet your annual financial objectives that means you should have approximately 1 sale each month.

We know, of course, that real estate doesn't really work like that and you might get two or three in one month and then not any for several months. Understanding, however, what your monthly budget requires to meet your objectives is critical to success.

Ask yourself what the requirements are for each week or drill down even further and ask yourself what is required each day to achieve that one-sale-a-month goal. As you begin to understand which methods of investing work best for you, you will begin to polish your skills to a point where you know exactly how many calls or contacts you must make to secure a solid opportunity. It isn't always perfect, but you should keep track of your calls and contacts at the beginning and when you secure a worthy investment opportunity count how many calls it took to achieve it. Do that the first two or three times. You will see that you likely have an average.

Let's say your average is one investment or sales opportunity every 15 calls or contacts. So, now you know that if you want to close 1 sale per month, you will need to make about 15 calls or contacts that month to achieve your goal. By taking the larger picture objectives and looking at your daily goal, you can both achieve the maximum and longer-term objective while making the process or method of achieving it very manageable.

Once we have completed a business plan and put your goals down on paper, they tend to become more real. Understanding how to break those goals into smaller sections so you can accomplish them makes the difference between being a success and being a failure. If your goals do seem very manageable to you in the daily "bite-size pieces," then you know that you have a plan that contains a foundation that can lead to success.

You do not want to set yourself up for failure. Establishing unrealistic goals in a business plan is a common mistake for a first time business owner of any type. If after you have broken your objectives into manageable activities and still find them difficult to attain, then perhaps your overall goals need revising.

This particular section of the book is about revisiting your business plan. As a small business owner and investor, you will always be learning something. You may find that 3 to 6 months from now the "strategy" you devised for your business is not the best way to approach future business. Trial and error, or as my grandfather used to say, "the school of hard knocks" is the best education you will ever receive. As you receive that education, the way you look at your business is going to change. It should change. Change in the business of investing is inevitable because the very market that we thrive on is changing every moment. As a result of either changes you want to make or changes that have come from other variables, your business plan will likely need changes.

The worst mistake you can make is to complete a business plan, put it in a one-half inch binder from the office supply store, file in on a shelf, and then never look at it again. You should be using the business plan as a system of checks and balances. To achieve success, you must be able to measure. And to measure, you must have something against which to measure. Your business plan should be a living checks and balances system for you. You will be grateful if you use it as the tool it can be and is intended to be.

If you ever need to seek capital funding or a bank loan in the future, your ability to measure yourself against your own objectives, and capable and flexible enough for making necessary changes on the fly, can go miles when it comes to a lender or capital investor making a financial support decision.

A living business plan is an example of your dedication to your company and your intelligence in relationship to good, old-fashioned business sense. Being able to alter your objectives on an as-needed basis to achieve greater rates of return and more dollars toward your bottom line is a business skill many believe can't be taught. I don't know about that . . . but I do know that it is something you need to teach yourself and something you will learn through dedication to the process.

Real Estate Investing

Real estate investing, more so than other self-employed businesses, includes many areas for learning. In a bakery, you must understand baked goods. In a beauty salon, you must understand the latest trends, styles, and methods for creating them.

In real estate investing, the things you must learn are generally more expansive than the two previous examples. You need to learn the methods of locating your opportunities, negotiating the sale through either the seller or the bank, you need to learn about general home construction so that you can identify costly problems in a property on site, and then you need to learn about the art of preparing the home for sale to achieve a quick return on your investment. And you must learn the art of doing a financial analysis on each of your potential investment properties, and you need to learn the ins-and-outs of depreciation and taxation laws for your particular situation.

More is involved in investing in real estate than opening a beauty salon or a bakery, but there is also a great deal more reward if you learn the layers and make the commitment to never assume you have learned it all. In this business, everyday there is something to learn.

Remember that the next time you pick up your business plan. Is it current? Does it contain the latest and greatest information to achieve long-term success for your company that you have in your head? If it's only in your head, and not in your plan, it may get lost when the next great piece of information, or idea, or education piles up on top of it.

Don't risk that chance. Look at it once a month and make sure it is right. If the plan is not right, then fix it. If you feel it is right, see if you can do anything to improve on it.

Tax Benefits

How tax savvy a businesswoman you are has a great effect on how much money is in your pocket at the end of the year. Tax codes allow you to deduct from your gross income costs for doing business. What you are left with is your net profit, otherwise referred to as net earnings. That amount is the amount that gets taxed, so the higher the number and the higher the taxes you pay. The lower that number, the lower the taxes. Obviously, deductions are paramount in keeping your dollars in your pockets.

As we have already established, knowing how to maximize your deductible business expenses lowers your taxable profit. When does the Internal Revenue Service (IRS) consider an expense a business tax-deductible expense?

Ordinary and Necessary Expenses

Section 162 of the Internal Revenue Code is the cornerstone for determining the tax deductibility of every business expenditure. Here are the first several words:

Trade or business expenses. (a) In general. There shall be allowed as a deduction all the ordinary and necessary expenses paid or incurred during the taxable year in carrying on any trade or business.

Section 162 goes on for what feels forever, but the important part is that expenses must be what is considered "ordinary and necessary" or they cannot be deducted. The tax code doesn't, however, define either what is ordinary or what is necessary. Luckily, in most cases, a legitimate business expense under section 162 is obvious, such as office supplies.

In some cases, such as travel, the IRS provides specific instructions for determining whether an expense is ordinary and necessary. This is often done through various IRS publications and regulations. It is entirely possible to get lost forever in the publications and regulations. Often one leads to another and so on. It's important to point out here that you will never entirely grasp all of the specific areas that apply to tax deductions. Some accountants and attorneys have invested their entire careers learning just that topic. If you don't understand a specific area, you are not alone—you are the majority, not the minority.

When a specific expense is not discussed in section 162 or in publications or regulations, federal courts have tried to figure out what Congress intended and apply it to a particular set of facts. The legal consensus is that ordinary and necessary refers to the purpose for which an expense is made. For example, having a cell phone plan is considered tax deductible for many businesses and their employees, but that is only accurate if those phones are being used to conduct business outside and away from normal office landlines. The courts have held that ordinary means "normal, common, and accepted under the circumstances by the business community." Necessary, on the other hand, is generally considered "appropriate and helpful."

Given those broad legal guidelines, it is not surprising that some folks have tried to push the envelope on ordinary and necessary business expenses. Be aware, however, that the IRS can push back at almost any time. Sometimes a compromise is reached, and sometimes the issue is thrown into a court's lap.

As ridiculous as it may sound, accountants and IRS professionals frequently rely on the "laugh test": Can you put down that business expense without laughing about putting one over on the IRS? If you can put it down and keep a straight face, then there may be some legitimacy to that expense. If you feel like you just got away with something by taking the deduction, you very likely may want to reconsider it because you won't actually know if you got away with it for quite some time.

Education Expenses

You can deduct education expenses if they are related to your current business, trade, or occupation. The expense must be to maintain or improve skills required in your present employment or be required by your employer or as a legal requirement of your job. The cost of education that qualifies you for a new job isn't deductible.

Legal and Professional Fees

Fees that you pay lawyers, tax professionals, or consultants generally can be deducted in the year incurred. But if the work clearly relates to future years, they must be deducted over the life of the benefit you get from the lawyer or other professional.

Business books, including those that help you do without legal and tax professionals, are fully deductible as a cost of doing business.

Bad Debts

If someone stiffs your business, the bad debt may or may not be deductible—it depends on the kind of product your business sells. See your accountant for more information.

If your business sells goods, you can deduct the cost of goods that you sell but aren't paid for. If, however, your business provides services, no deduction is allowed for time you devote to a client or customer who didn't pay. The rationale behind that rule is because it would be too easy for businesses to inflate bills and claim large deductions for bad debts.

Business Entertaining

If you pick up the tab for entertaining present or prospective customers, you may deduct 50 percent of the cost if it is either:

•directly related to the business and business is discussed at the event—for example, a catered meeting at your office, or

•associated with the business, and the entertainment takes place immediately before or after a business discussion.

On the receipt or bill, always make a note of the specific business purpose -- for example, "Lunch with Joyce Slater of Ace Manufacturing Company to discuss widget contract."

Travel

When you travel for business you can deduct many expenses including the cost of plane fare, costs of operating your vehicle, taxis, lodging, meals, shipping business materials, clothes cleaning, telephone calls, faxes, and tips. What about combining business and pleasure? It's okay, as long as business is the primary purpose of the trip. But if you take your family long, you can deduct only your own expenses, just as if you had traveled alone. The adjoining hotel room and the amusement park tickets might catch the auditor's eye.

If you've got some old computers or office furniture, giving it to a school or nonprofit organization can yield goodwill plus a tax benefit. But if the equipment has been fully depreciated (written off), you can't claim a deduction.

Taxes

Taxes incurred in operating your business are generally deductible. How and when they are deducted depends on the type of tax.

- sales tax on items you buy for your business's day-to-day operations is deductible as part of the cost of the items and not deducted separately. But tax on a big business asset, such as a vehicle, must be added to the vehicle's cost basis. Tax on the asset is not deductible entirely in the year the vehicle was bought.

- Excise and fuel taxes are separately deductible expenses.

- If your business pays employment taxes; the employer's share is deductible as a business expense. Self-employment tax is paid by individuals, not their businesses, and so isn't a business expense.

- Federal income tax paid on business income is never deductible. State income tax can be deducted on your federal return as an itemized deduction, not as a business expense.

- Real estate tax on property used for business is deductible, along with any special local assessments for repairs or maintenance. If the assessment is for an improvement—for example, to build a sidewalk—it isn't immediately deductible. Instead, it is deducted over a period of years.

Advertising and Promotion
The cost of ordinary advertising of your goods or services, such as business cards or yellow page ads, is a deductible expense. Promotional costs that create business goodwill, for example, sponsoring a football team, are also deductible as long as there is a clear connection between the sponsorship and your business. For example, naming the team the "The Mini Investors" or listing the business name in the program is evidence of the promotion effort.

Easily Overlooked Business Expenses

Here are some additional routine deductions that many business owners miss. Keep your eye out for them.

- ☐ audiotapes and videotapes related to business skills
- ☐ bank service charges
- ☐ business association dues
- ☐ business gifts
- ☐ business-related magazines and books
- ☐ casual labor and tips
- ☐ casualty and theft losses
- ☐ coffee and beverage service
- ☐ commissions
- ☐ consultant fees
- ☐ credit bureau fees
- ☐ office supplies

- ☐ online computer services related to business
- ☐ parking and meters
- ☐ petty cash funds
- ☐ postage
- ☐ promotion and publicity
- ☐ seminars and trade shows
- ☐ taxi and bus fare
- ☐ telephone calls away from the business

Note: Just because you didn't get a receipt does not mean you can't deduct the expense, so keep track of those small items and get big tax savings.

Conclusion

It would take a lot more than 13 chapters to cover all there is to cover about real estate investing and that if you take that chance you will see infinite rewards. Making a real estate dollar is not the hardest dollar you will have made to this point in your life, and it is likely not ever going to be the hardest dollar you make going forward. Granted, you will have to stretch your wings and learn new things, but once you have mastered those areas you will be able to bring home the real estate investment dollar today.

Another great aspect of real estate investing is that there is no glass ceiling. In real estate investing, not only can you see the sky but also you can do what it takes to reach it without anyone telling you that you can't and without bumping your head on the inevitable corporate glass ceiling that you didn't see coming.

Believe in yourself and that will take you farther than anything you learned in this book and anything you will learn about real estate investing going forward. Believe in yourself. I believe in you!

Please give this book an honest review on Amazon.

Thank you for your purchase!

www.ingramcontent.com/pod-product-compliance
Lightning Source LLC
Chambersburg PA
CBHW050207230526
45470CB00001B/281